Traditional Samplers

Traditional Samplers

The world's most beautiful samplers for you to make at home

Regina Forstner

THORSONS PUBLISHING GROUP

First UK Edition published in 1988

First published by Rosenheimer Verlagshaus Alfred Forg GmbH & Co.,
8200 Rosenheim, Germany

© Regina Forstner 1983
English text © Thorsons Publishing Group 1989
Pattern illustrations © Eva Mauracher 1983

British Library Cataloguing in Publication Data

Forstner, Regina
Traditional samplers: the world's most beautiful
samplers for you to make at home.
1. Embroidery, Samplers
I. Title
746.44
ISBN 0-7225-1813-7

*Published by Thorsons Publishers Limited,
Wellingborough, Northamptonshire NN8 2RQ, England*

Printed in Italy by G. Canale & C. S.p.A., Turin

1   3   5   7   9   10   8   6   4   2

Contents

Acknowledgements

Translated by Anne Davenport
Craft Editor, Eileen Lowcock
Photographs by Gerhard Trumler
Illustrations by Eva Mauracher

The use of cross stitch and patterns

The cross stitch was known to the ancient Egyptians and was such a central part of their day-to-day lives that embroidery frames were put into the tombs of aristocratic ladies. The Romans too were adept with their needles and the author Pliny mentions the artistic needlework produced at this time.

Cross stitch was probably used so frequently because it is such an easy stitch to work and has so many applications. Indeed, examples of cross stitch patterns can be found almost world wide: in Egypt, Iran, the Balkans, the Iberian peninsula and in countries throughout Europe.

As well as being easy to do, the cross stitch was considered to bring good luck and to keep away evil. It was therefore very popular in folk art. It can be found decorating christening shawls, cradle covers, trousseaus, bed linen, altar cloths and clerical robes.

The Tree of Life is often represented in the form of stylized flowers such as carnations and tulips. Often stags, birds or even dragons are embroidered as guardians of the Tree of Life with hearts and vases being used as symbols to represent the vessel of the waters of life.

Floral and figurative motifs decorated the hems of dresses, children's clothes, aprons, scarves, shawls, shirt collars, blouses, sleeves, cuffs, tablecloths, table napkins, hand towels, ornamental cushions, cushion covers, counterpanes, handkerchiefs, pin cushions, book covers, comb cases, spectacle cases, tobacco pouches, cigarette lighter cases and pocket books or, they were framed and hung on the wall.

The cross stitch patterns in this book have been specially selected to inspire you to decorate all sorts of items, beautifully. If you wanted to make a gift, for example, you could make a lovely present by embroidering a beautiful rose, carnation or forget-me-not (page 48) on a white linen handkerchief. Or you could decorate a table cloth for your breakfast table with a coffee pot and mill as corner motifs (page 73). Lovely rows of flower patterns (pages 46 and 47), could also be used or you could use them to make a fine linen tablecloth the perfect foil for your best china. The animal motifs are perfect for decorating a child's bed linen. One animal, such as the parrot, or a whole row of them embroidered on the pillow case, top edge of the sheet, duvet cover or bedspread look absolutely charming.

Try wreaths of flowers too with the date stitched into the centre of the design (page 43), a colourful cornucopia (pages 42 and 75), a horse (page 40), or a St Bernard dog (page 53), worked into a lovely picture and framed. All these designs make such beautiful presents that you will probably find it very hard to part with them but, hopefully, you will have gained such pleasure from working the embroidery that you will quickly produce some more lovely things or work on a beautiful sampler.

I hope too that this collection of cross stitch patterns will inspire you to not only copy them but to create your own designs. Let yourself be carried away from the hurly burly of everyday pressures. Relax and enjoy the enchanting embroidery patterns collected here for you.

The history of cross stitch

The period between 1815 and 1848 was a golden age for embroidery. It was very fashionable for embroidery to decorate clothes, furniture, table and bed linen, be made into pictures and so on.

The embroideries were largely worked by the middle class – or, to be more precise, by middle-class women and girls. As middle-class women and girls were denied any professional occupation outside the home, they had plenty of free time and it was deemed appropriate to their class that they fill it with some artistic occupation.

Young girls were taught needlework, painting, drawing, piano playing and singing and it was useful at that time to do delicate needlework at social occasions such as family gatherings, tea parties or during conversation in the drawing room. Thus needlework played an important role in social life. The craftsmanship of the tools they used testify to this: needle cases of ivory and silver and beautiful embroidery frames.

At the very beginning of the nineteenth century, women preferred whitework embroidery, but during the first half of the century it became fashionable to embroider cross stitch in colours – so popular, in fact, that it finally replaced whitework embroidery altogether in popularity. It was not only the samplers, handed down from generation to generation, that encouraged cross stitch, but the newly-invented lithography made it possible to produce colourful embroidery pattern books in large numbers. Thus cross stitch flourished. Ideas on sensitivity and romanticism are frequently reflected in the cross stitch patterns. Ladies embroidered tender dedications such as 'With Love', 'In memory', 'In remembrance', with their name and the date. Often they made a wreath of colourful flowers, the initials of the names of the flowers spelling out the word 'Friendship'. Very popular too, were all kinds of patterns with flowers, featured either singly or in sprays or made into bouquets, as well as scenes from rural life.

The history of the sampler

The sampler is one of the most important types of textile work because it shows exactly how the different kinds of stitches and patterns were worked, for collecting, recording, preserving and handing them down to the next generation.

The samplers were made from the most varied of materials. Linen was the most frequently used, followed by wool and later canvas. These materials were good grounds on which to practise cross stitch and for collecting together mainly flower patterns, animal motifs and figures.

The patterns were collected so avidly because, as you will recall, it was very fashionable during the first half of the nineteenth century to ornament all objects suitable for embroidery such as pillow cases, bedspreads, tablecloths, napkins and so on. But the sampler was more important than mere decoration. It was also the best way to develop familiarity with the most diverse motifs. However, that said, most of the samplers you can see in museums were certainly not practice pieces. They were, rather, demonstrations of skill in varieties of stitches and patterns that had previously been practised on remnants or small scraps of fabric. A sure eye for arranging patterns harmoniously was needed too for the sampler to be a success.

Repeatedly, individual samplers stand out because of a particularly beautifully embroidered selection of patterns and beause they have been arranged in such a well-balanced way. We assume that these pieces were made by adults; either by teachers as models for their pupils, or as a pattern to be copied by professional embroiderers.

Once a woman or young girl completed a sampler, she did not put it away out of sight. Instead, she had it mounted or framed so that she could hang it on the wall as a decoration. In the late eighteenth century and especially in the nineteenth century, it was traditional to mount the sampler with paper or silk ribbons (see the cover) and then display it or use it as a model.

The samplers became heirlooms, handed down from generation to generation, and a daughter's sampler was displayed with that of her mother's and eventually the granddaughter's was added also.

The oldest known sampler dates from about 850 AD and was found in Chinese Turkestan. It is a square piece of cloth 25 by 30 cm (10 by 12 inches), embroidered with 28 different patterns. It is true that thirteenth to fifteenth century samplers from the Asiatic area have been preserved, but whether or not a continual tradition developed after this time cannot be verified.

In Europe, where samplers were produced in almost every country, the oldest examples date back to the late sixteenth and early seventeenth century. We can draw on pictorial and written sources as well as on these surviving samplers for information about the methods and traditions of earlier centuries. One pictorial source goes back to the fourteenth century to Villafranca del Panades, to the Church of San Francisco in Spain. There, on a panel, are portrayed seven temple virgins (among them Mary), showing their embroideries to an older woman. Another source is the painting of the Holy Family by Joose van Cleve (1485–1540), which can be dated to about 1520. In it we see Mary the Mother, who is looking after the child Jesus and who has therefore put aside her embroidery. On the table is a folded sampler on which we can see carnations and other floral ornaments and a representation of an animal, either a lion or a dog. On the right are silk threads rolled upon cards, and the threaded needle is still stuck in a ball of thread.

However, written sources come mainly from England, and from as early as the sixteenth century. There is also evidence for the popularity and knowledge of samplers. They are mentioned in housekeeping records and inventories – even in wills. The oldest written source mentioning samplers also comes from England. The following note was entered in the account book of Elizabeth of York on 10th July 1502 'an for an eine of lynnyn cloth for a sampler for the Queen.'

We must not draw the misleading conclusion that England was the birthplace of the sampler. However, compared with European examples, the samplers are very well worked. Also, written evidence was collected in England much earlier than in the rest of Europe and the tradition of making samplers was continued.

When and where the first samplers were made in Europe has not been established, so these questions must remain unanswered. However, it can be assumed that the first samplers were made in the European countries that had contact with the peoples of the Asiatic countries, from whom they learned the art of embroidery and, hence, the making of samplers. The samplers, in turn, became part of their cultural heritage.

Nevertheless, when we consider that the daughters of the nobility and rich bourgeois were taught needlework in convent schools from the eighth century, it is amazing that in Europe only samplers dating from the late sixteenth and early seventeenth centuries have survived. No samplers have survived from the Middle Ages nor are there any sources, whether pictorial or written, that point to the existence of such samplers.

In the sixteenth century, needlework experienced a golden age, since it had become the fashion to decorate clothing with embroidery and lace. Some of the samplers that have survived from this and the seventeenth centuries were certainly used only for collecting patterns. Not every embroiderer could afford the expensive pattern books with the printed patterns and so samplers served as their pattern books. Besides, pattern books were not very durable at first so people simply embroidered, in some order, various patterns, edgings, numerals and letters onto a piece of linen so as to have it on hand when they needed it.

The oldest surviving samplers from the early seventeenth century are almost always long and narrow because the looms of the time were very narrow. The advantage of this, however, was the sampler could be rolled up and kept in a sewing basket when it was not being used. Often a sampler was made from several pieces of cloth sewn together. They rarely have a date on them, since they were worked on over a period of years – pattern being added to pattern, all jumbled up, forming a genuine collection built up over time. On the early examples edgings and corner patterns appear side by side and well represented, too, are religious themes such as the Easter Lamb, the Crucifixion and Saint George fighting the dragon. Frequent secular themes are courting couples and animals. These examples were embroidered with silk and linen thread.

Towards the end of the seventeenth century and during the eighteenth century the examples are mostly several samplers sewn together and are therefore relatively large. They were mostly embroidered with fine woollen thread. Typical of this period are patterns that completely cover the fabric, mostly embroidered on coarse linen. Occasionally, small patterns of silk embroidery are added. The patterns on these samplers are intended almost exclusively for furniture covers for example, acanthus sprays, designs with large flowers, tassled edgings, loop designs and geometric patterns such as wavy or zig-zag patterns, lattice work, plaited edgings and Solomon's knots.

What is interesting is that the embroiderer could use a wide range of colours to create shading and give an impression of space; at times up to five different shades of one colour have been used. But, if you compare different samplers with each other, you can see that they have often the same combinations of colour and pattern, only the size is different, and this of course depends on the fabric used. In addition to flower and geometric patterns, animal representations such as hares, birds and stags also featured in embroideries used in the home.

All the colours appear in every imaginable shade, ranging from the very palest pink to the darkest red, from the lightest yellow to the darkest green and from the palest blue to deep indigo.

Considering the wide range of colours and stitches that were used, such as cross stitch, Renaissance stitch, Gobelin stitch and satin stitch, it is natural to assume that in this case it was not housewives and young girls who made such samplers for home use, but professional embroiderers, perhaps during their apprenticeship.

Later in the eighteenth century we again find the narrow pieces of linen, with patterns arranged at random, through which the background fabric shows. The familiar Renaissance motifs are still used, but the influence of the Rococo can already be seen. Significantly, fewer ornaments are embroidered, but a lot more figures. The more complicated stitches have almost ceased to be used and cross stitch in its different forms begins its triumphant progress. The use of cross stitch exclusively in turn calls for a more strict arrangement of patterns, so that flowing lines disappeared, and human figures are almost always embroidered viewed from the front.

The samplers usually include motifs such as alphabets, edging patterns, the date and the initials of the embroiderer. In the centre of the sampler, sometimes the Crucifixion is embroidered, and near it Adam and Eve under the Tree of Life, along with various animals such as a stag, crab, horse or parrot. Views of castles and of course, flower motifs also feature in the samplers.

The colours most frequently used in the late eighteenth century were pale shades in such colours as flesh tones, yellow and green and rarely do we see red or black being used.

Only in the nineteenth century was there once again a powerful and original use of colour in samplers. Black, red and blue were introduced. The first half of the nineteenth century brought into fashion not only bright colours but also a new fabric for embroidery, wool. This, like the linen, was sold in narrow widths but was woven especially for samplers. The embroidery thread the embroiderer's used now was silk.

The arrangement of the patterns, especially those on the edges, that had followed a precise order well into the eighteenth century began to alter completely during the late nineteenth century. The embroiderers began to scatter the motifs, now almost exclusively figures, over the fabric, which was square rather than long and narrow, and the arrangement of the motifs was completely a matter of personal taste. The alphabets, which dis-appeared almost completely from the samplers were embroidered on separate strips of fabric.

A visible decline in the standard of the embroideries set in during the second half of the nineteenth century. Samplers were embroidered in garish colours using large stitches and so looked rather coarse.

The embroidering of samplers continued up to the start of the first World War and then declined once more. Now it is incredibly fashionable with such creative geniuses as Kaffe Fasset taking the craft to new aesthetic heights. Traditional samplers are worked with great care and are a consuming hobby for embroiderers of all ages. They are made and framed as pictures or used as cushion covers, bags, rugs and all kinds of other beautiful, durable things and will without doubt become the heirlooms of tomorrow.

Embroidery patterns

As well as samplers, which were, of course, the best and clearest way of retaining patterns, the oldest needlework patterns to be found in Europe are recorded in pattern books. These pattern books, used for collecting and passing on patterns, have been known in Germany, England, France and Italy since the early sixteenth century. The patterns in them were set out and sold first in the form of wood cuts then later as engravings. They show ornaments as well as representations of animals, man and nature, which could be worked with different embroidery stitches, but were mainly meant for cross stitch work, since the patterns are mostly laid out on squared paper.

Towards the end of the eighteenth century, magazines appeared everywhere on the market with instructions for needlework and pages of embroidery patterns.

It is interesting that many motifs from the pattern books of the sixteenth and seventeenth centuries lived on into the nineteenth century. Thus we find in samplers from the last century the representation of the Easter Lamb or Saint George fighting the dragon, and also the courting pair and the stag. The old pattern books must have been highly regarded for centuries and in continuous use.

Frequently, the pattern books contained some almost empty pages, with only squares printed on them, to allow the individual embroiderers to draw in their own patterns.

The motifs

There are two main types of motif: religious and secular.

Among the religious motifs, which predominate on samplers until about 1815, are representations of the Crucifixion, or the Lamb of God with the banner of the resurrection, of Adam and Eve beneath the Tree of Life, St Peter's cockerel, Mary, the chalice, the monstrance and also the initials of Jesus Christ. There are some splendid examples of these, mainly on samplers from the later Renaissance and the early Baroque periods.

Between 1815 and 1848, secular motifs replace religious ones. A wealth of sentimental patterns and romantic ideas come onto the scene and these were reflected in the samplers worked during this time. Flowers are among the favourite patterns and the rose took first place. The rose, the queen of flowers, was either embroidered singly or multiplied and made into beautiful bouquets or wreaths or woven into garlands. Roses were worked in delicate, gradated shades and combined with five forget-me-nots, carnations, tulips, oak leaves and branches of laurel. The most popular patterns featured flowers in wreaths, sprays, vases, cornucopiae in bright colours, little temples, urns and trees, such as weeping willows. All these motifs can be found on the pages of books and on greetings cards of the period.

In addition to the floral motifs, animals such as dogs, horses, cats, hares, stags, sheep, crabs, squirrels and birds, especially parrots, cockerels, cranes and peacocks were popular. Parrots had become fashionable since the eighteenth century and the peacock was often kept as a domestic animal on farms during the eighteenth and nineteenth centuries. City gates, houses, household items, furniture, ships, anchors and hearts were also recurring motifs.

All these motifs appeared over an astonishingly wide geographical area and the subjects and style of execution were used without much change over long periods of time.

Practical matters

Fabric

The best fabric for cross stitch embroidery was and still is linen. This is because the weave is very even. This not only has the advantage of making it easy to count the threads, but means that the finished embroidery will not be distorted. However, in the nineteenth century woollen fabric was also used and canvas was a popular ground as well. Canvas is a coarsely woven cotton material, the weave of which makes the counting of the threads easier and, therefore, it was preferred by embroiderers in the second half of the nineteenth century.

It is best these days to use either even-weave linen, cotton or woollen fabric. The important thing to look for when choosing a fabric for the embroidery is that the weave is suitable for thread counting. Avoid dress and upholstery fabrics since the weave in these cannot be relied upon to be of an accurate, even weave, thus the finished stitch and pattern will be distorted.

The cross stitch

Cross stitch is constructed by lying two threads crosswise over each other. In Denmark and America, the lower thread slants from lower left to upper right and is then crossed from lower right to upper left, as shown in the diagram. Throughout the rest of Europe, stitches are traditionally worked from lower right to upper left, then crossed from lower left to upper right. It makes no difference, however, which way you stitch, as long as all the stitiches are crossed in the same direction. If there are several adjacent stitches of the same colour, one slant of the cross stitch is worked first, then worked back across to finish the cross stitch.

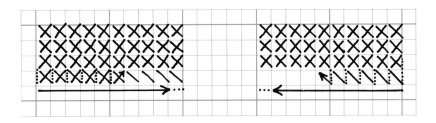

Needle and thread

The embroidery needle must be compatible with the thickness of the fabric and the embroidery thread. This means that the embroidery needle, the embroidery thread and the thread of the fabric to be embroidered must, as far as possible, be of the same thickness. The simplest thing to do is to match the thickness of the embroidery thread to the fabric. This can be done without difficulty if you use only embroidery thread. We recommend that, whenever you can, you use Coats Stranded Embroidery Cotton. This thread results in all embroidery with a fine, flat surface, which imitates very closely the texture of the original samplers. Shiny mercerized yarns are less suitable.

For very fine fabrics I recommend a pointed needle known as a crewel needle, although usually a needle with a rounded point – a tapestry needle – is better to work with because it does not split the threads of the fabric you are embroidering. The basic principle is that the finer the fabric (embroidery thread and needle), the finer the embroidered pattern will be.

Patterns

Genuine cross stitch patterns are always counted patterns and should never be printed on the fabric. The colours shown in the pattern section have been matched to the original historic samplers using the Coats Stranded Embroidery Cotton range and the shade numbers are given for those of you who would like to recreate the beautiful and fashionable look of the traditional sampler. Copying the pattern exactly is also made much easier. I tried to get as close as possible to the original colours, still unspoiled by yellowing and fading. Of course it is equally possible to make your own choice of colours according to your own taste and imagination. You may, for instance, like the fashionable faded look and decide to work the sampler in paler colours or choose to arrange the patterns to your own composition – the possibilities are endless!

Sampler dated 1812, worked in silk on a linen ground. Note the strictly geometric patterned edgings.

Part of a sampler, made in the golden age of embroidery in about 1830. It, too, is worked in silk on linen.

Right *This sampler was made in 1838 and shows the very typical flower edgings. It is worked in silk on linen.*

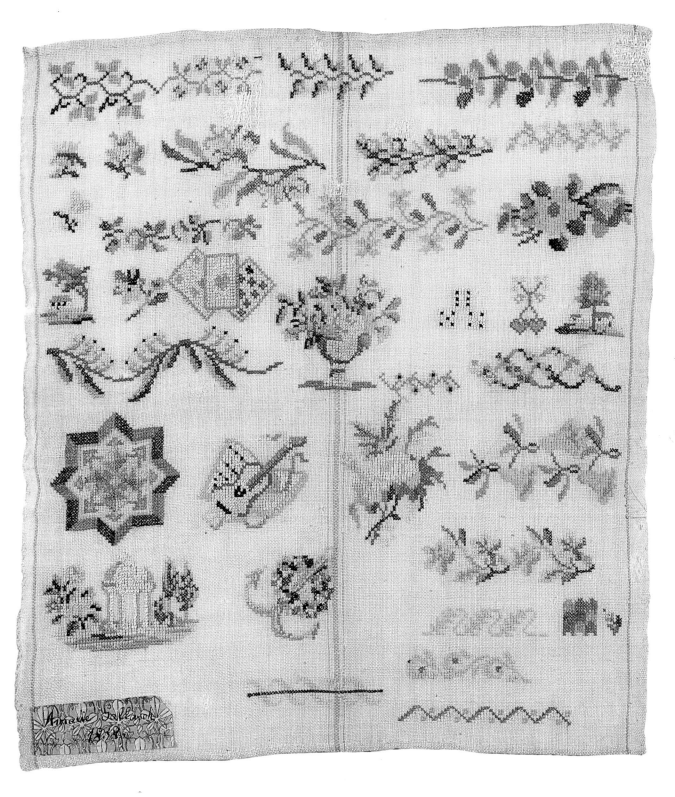

In this sampler, dated 1847, the emphasis is on the alphabets. They are very decorative even though they are also very simple.

Right *A partial view of an 1820 sampler, embroidered with silk thread on linen. The strict, almost geometrical arrangement of the motifs is typical of this time.*

A sampler from about 1820. It is embroidered in silk on linen.

Right *This is a part of an 1821 sampler worked in silk on linen. Notice the beautiful rose edging in Gobelin style.*

A vase of flowers from 1847 in silk on linen.

A cornucopia from about 1820 in silk on linen.

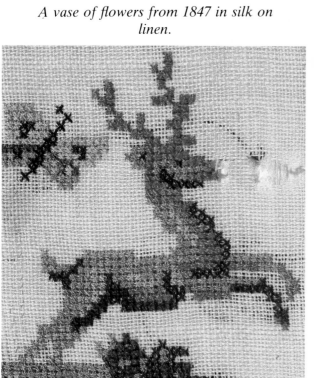

A stag from about 1823 in silk on linen.

A parrot from about 1812 in silk on cambric.

Pattern designs

Peacock motif from 1812
(see page 25)

Wreath of flowers from about 1820
(see page 30)

Coronet from 1812
(see page 25)

■ = black (403)   O = pale blue (128)

⊟ = silver grey (397)   ⊗ = violet (873)

△ = yellow (290)   X = reddish pink (29)

◈ = medium green (244) Z = pink (25)

◇ = light green (242)   ∧ = pale pink (23)

(*Note:* Coats Stranded Embroidery Cotton shade number is given in brackets after the colour name)

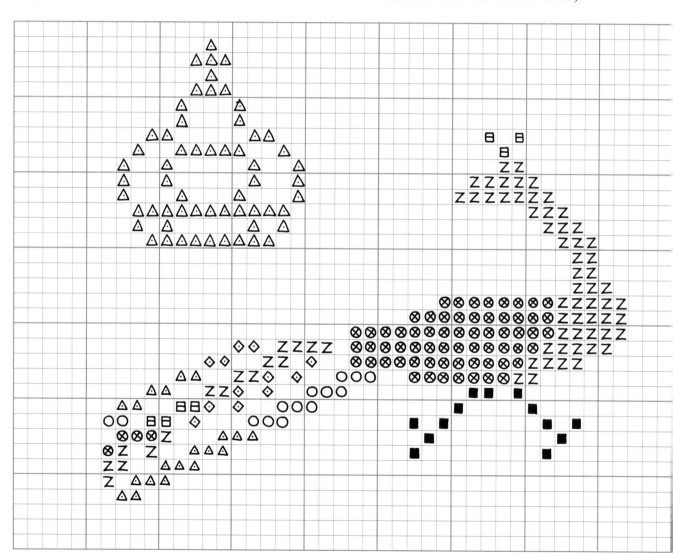

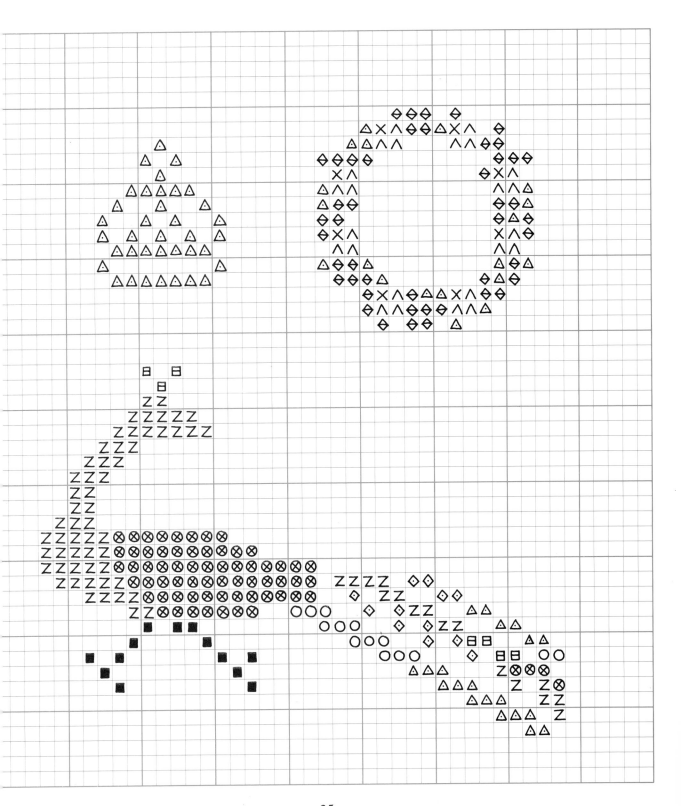

Flower motifs from about 1820
(see page 30)

Cockerel from 1812
(see page 25)

Bird from 1812
(see page 25)

■ = black (403)   ● = dark blue (150)
▲ = medium brown (371) Φ = medium blue (132)
△ = yellow (290)   ☉ = light blue (130)
◆ = dark green (246) Z = pink (25)
⬥ = medium green (244) ∧ = pale pink (23)

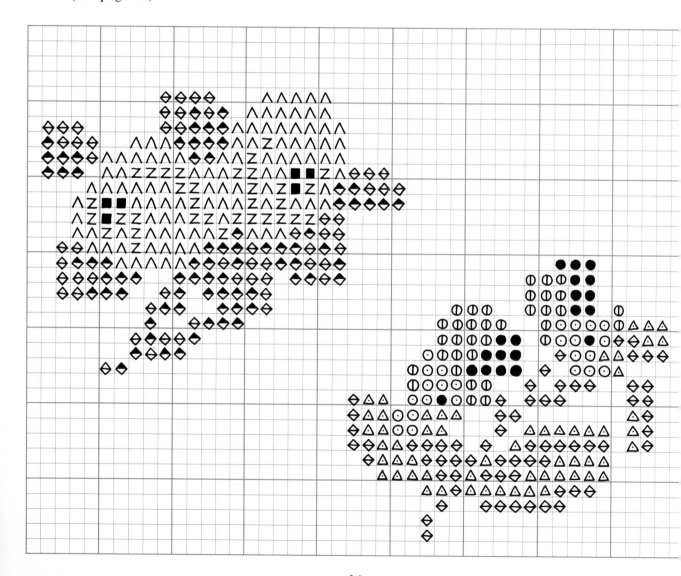

36

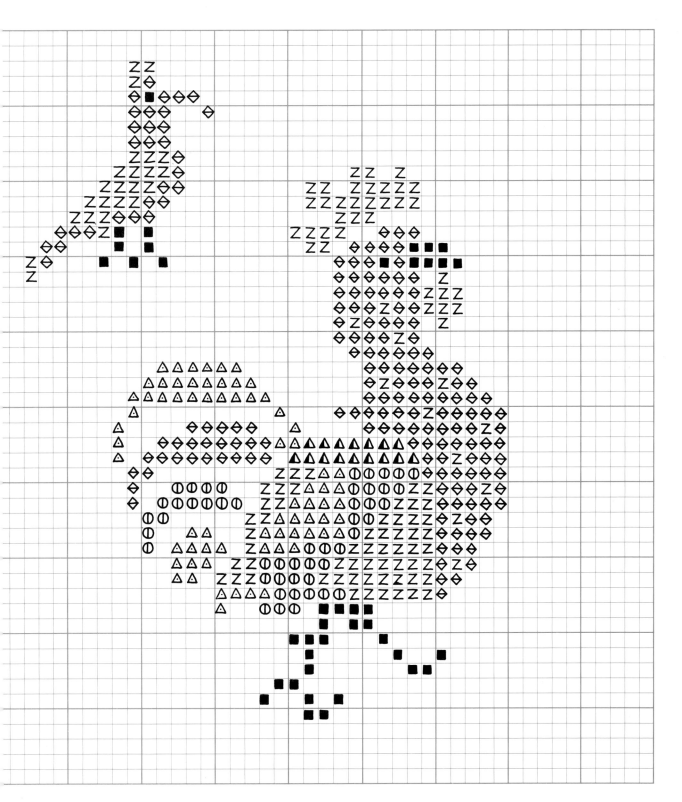

Flower motif and lamb from about 1820

(see page 30)

■ = black (403)   ◈ = dark green (246)
⊟ = silver grey (397)   ◇ = medium green (244)
□ = white (402)   ⊙ = light blue (130)
△ = yellow (290)   Z = pink (25)

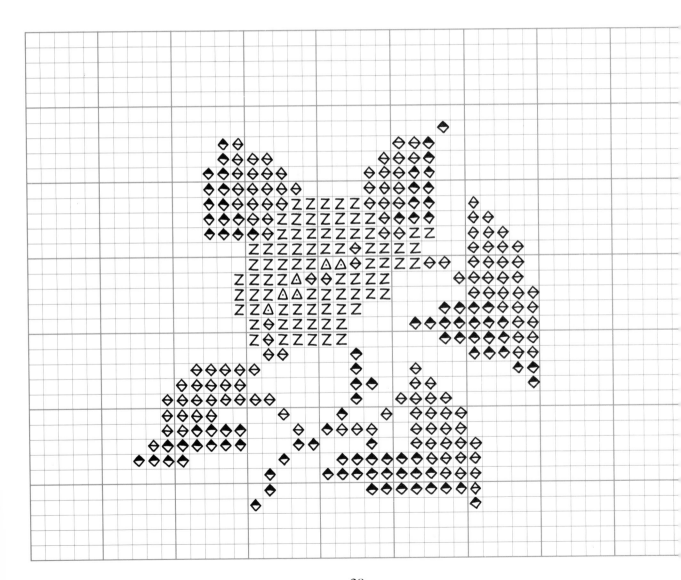

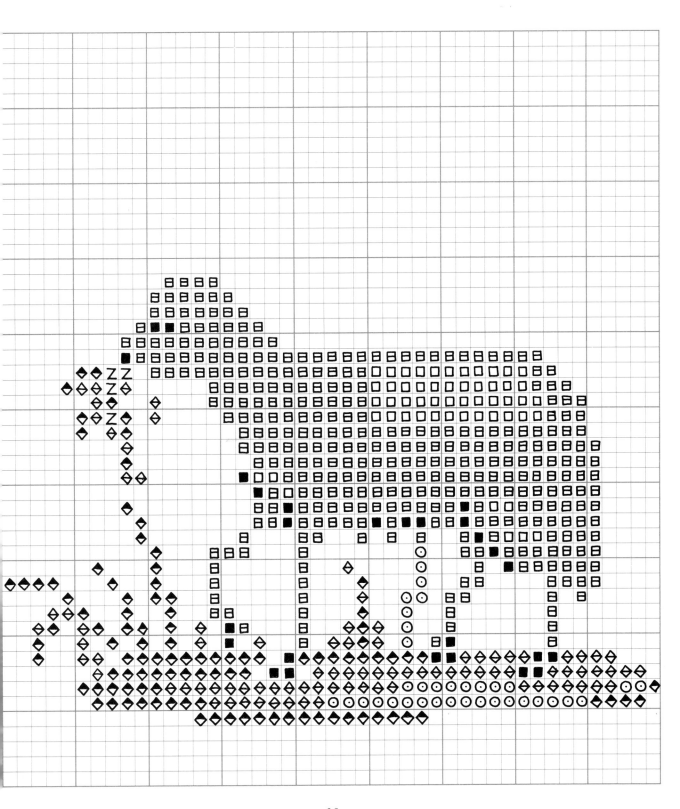

Horse from about 1820
(see page 30)

Rider and sun from 1821
(see page 31)

- ■ = black (403)
- □ = white (402)
- ▲ = dark brown (360)
- ◮ = light brown (369)
- △ = dark yellow (291)
- △ = yellow (290)
- ◈ = dark green (246)
- ◈ = medium green (244)
- ◇ = light green (242)
- ⊙ = light blue (130)
- ✕ = reddish pink (29)
- Z = pink (25)

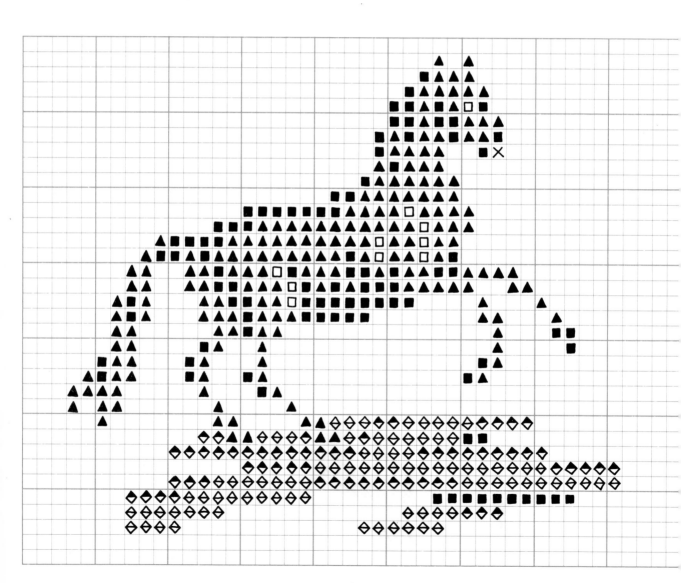

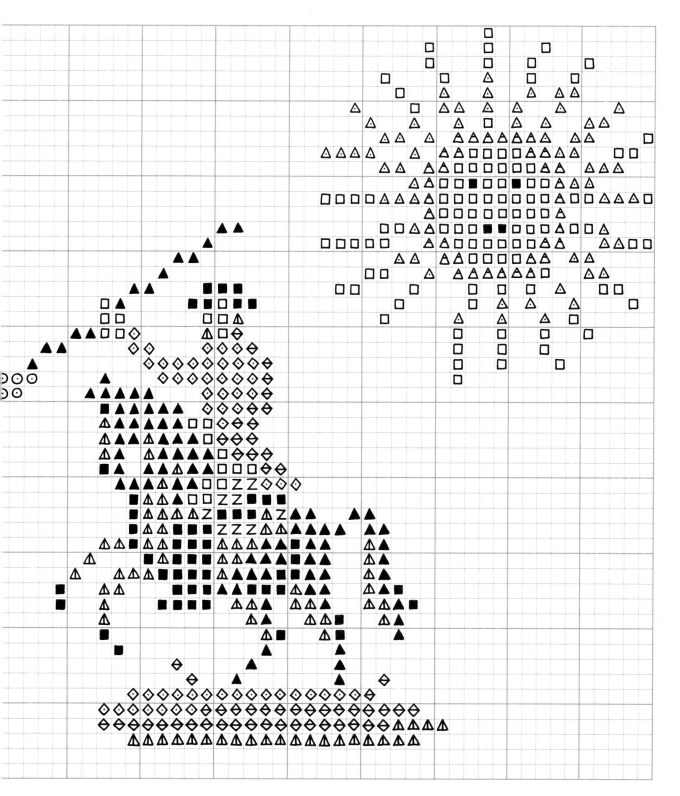

Cornucopia from about 1820
(see pages 30 and 32)

Wreath of flowers from 1821
(see page 31)

■ = black (403)

▲ = dark brown (360)

△ = yellow (290)

⬖ = dark green (246)

⬖ = medium green (244)

◇ = light green (242)

⏀ = medium blue (132)

⊙ = light blue (130)

Z = pink (25)

X = reddish pink (29)

∧ = pale pink (23)

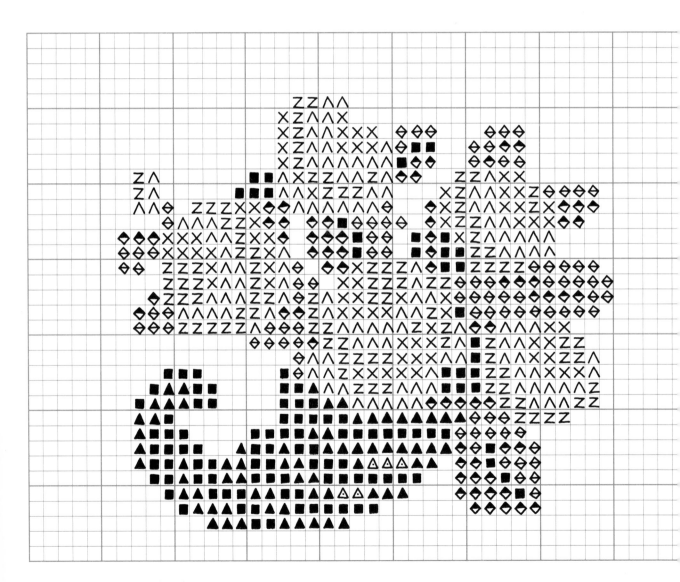

42

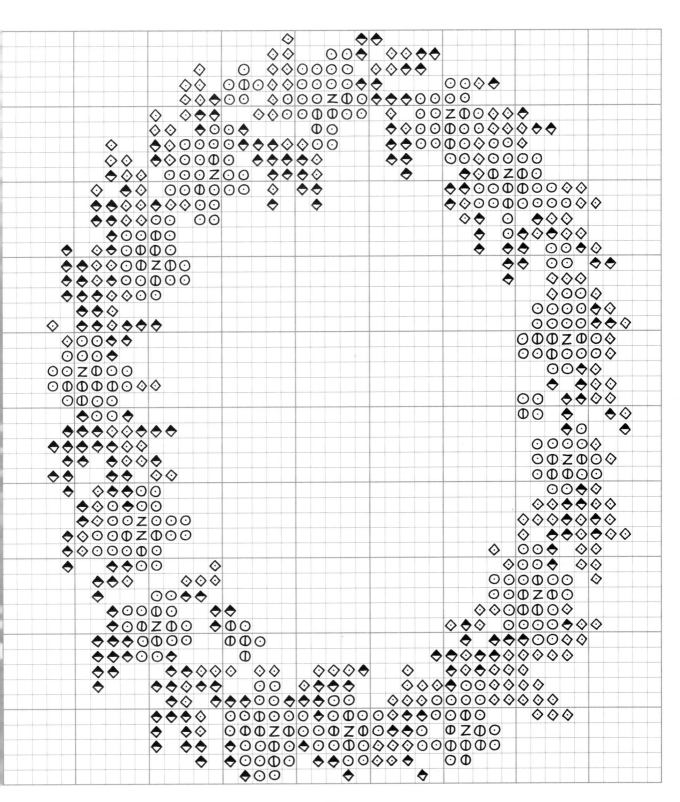

Flower motifs from about 1820
(see page 30)

Gondola and moon from 1821
(see page 31)

Motif with hearts from 1838
(see page 27)

■ = black (403)   ☉ = light blue (130)
□ = white (402)   Φ = medium blue (13⬤
▲ = medium brown (371)   Z = pink (25)
△ = yellow (290)   ∧ = pale pink (23)
◆ = dark green (246)   ✛ = red (47)
◈ = medium green (244)   X = reddish pink (29)
◇ = light green (242)

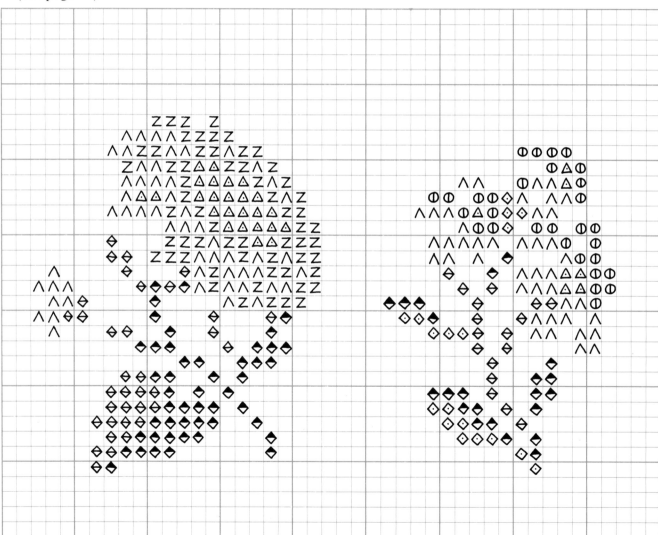

44

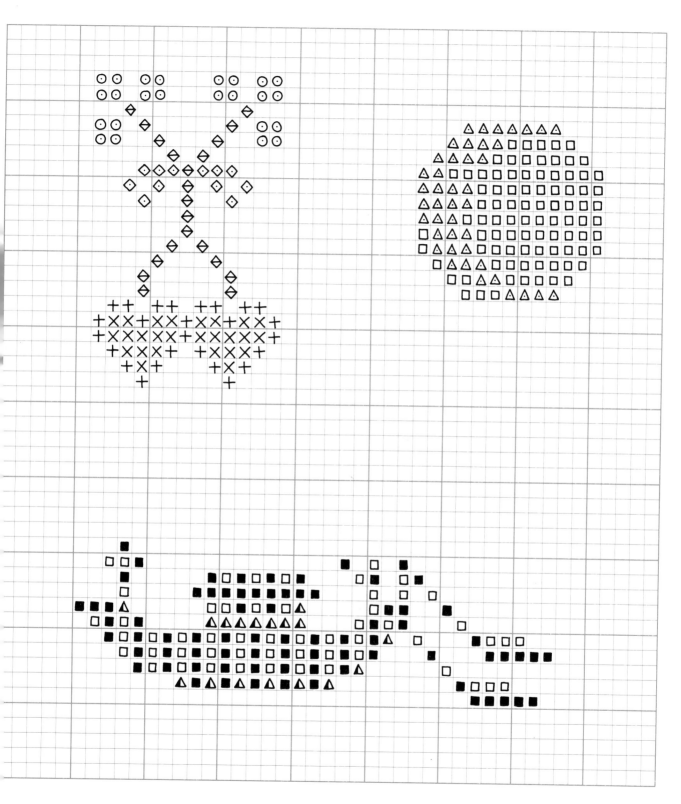

Rows of patterns from 1821

(see page 31)

□ = white (402)   ◆ = turquoise (187)
▲ = light brown (369)   ◑ = medium blue (132)
△ = dark yellow (291)   ☉ = light blue (130)
◆ = dark green (246)   ○ = pale blue (128)
⊖ = medium green (244)   Z = pink (25)
◇ = light green (242)   ∧ = pale pink (23)

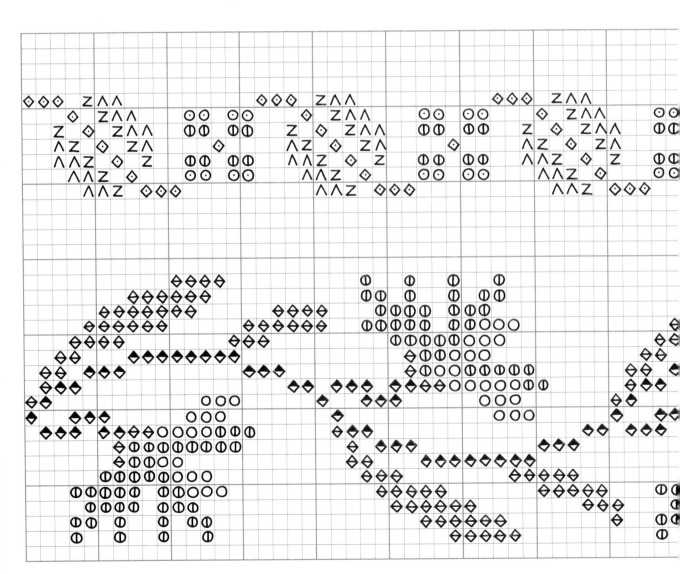

46

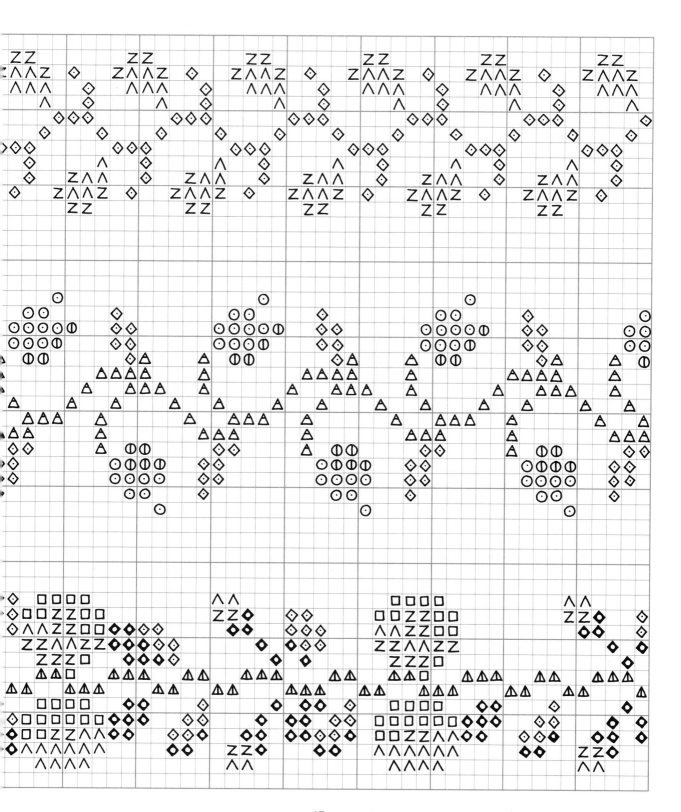

Rows of patterns from 1921 Forget-me-not and row patterns from 1823
(cover)

◆ = dark green (246)   ⊙ = light blue (130)
⬖ = medium green (244)   ○ = pale blue (128)
◇ = light green (242)   ⊗ = violet (873)
▲ = dark yellow (291)   + = red (47)
△ = yellow (290)   Z = pink (25)
● = dark blue (135)   ∧ = pale pink (23)
◐ = medium blue (132)

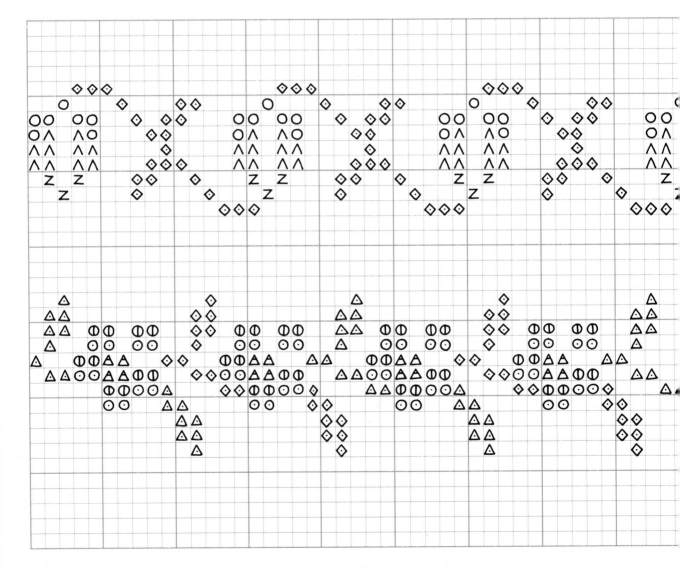

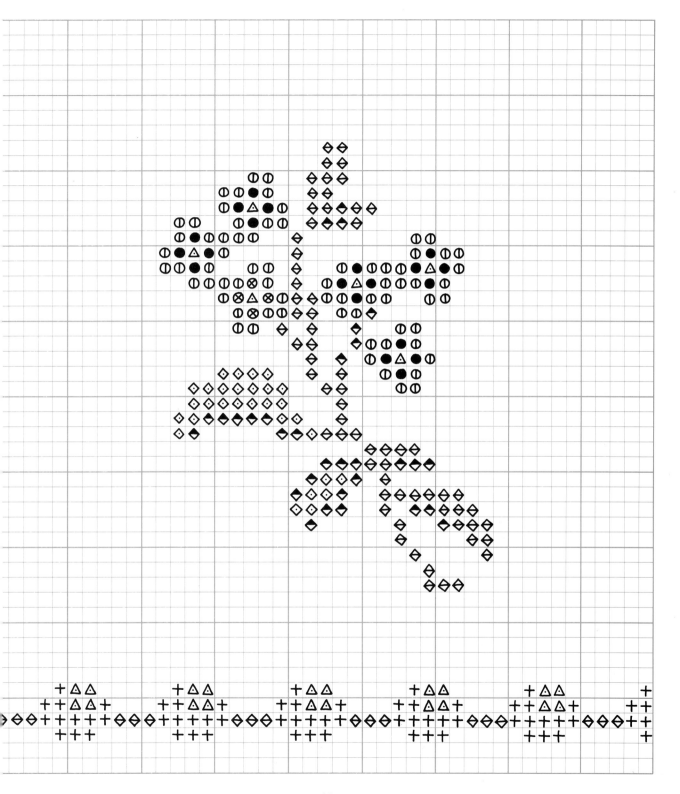

Squirrel from 1830, cockerel and stag from 1823
(see pages 26, 32 and cover)

■ = black (403)
□ = medium grey (399)
▲ = dark brown (360)
◬ = medium brown (371)
⬘ = light brown (369)

◆ = dark green (246)
⬥ = medium green (244)
⊙ = light blue (130)
+ = red (47)
Z = pink (25)

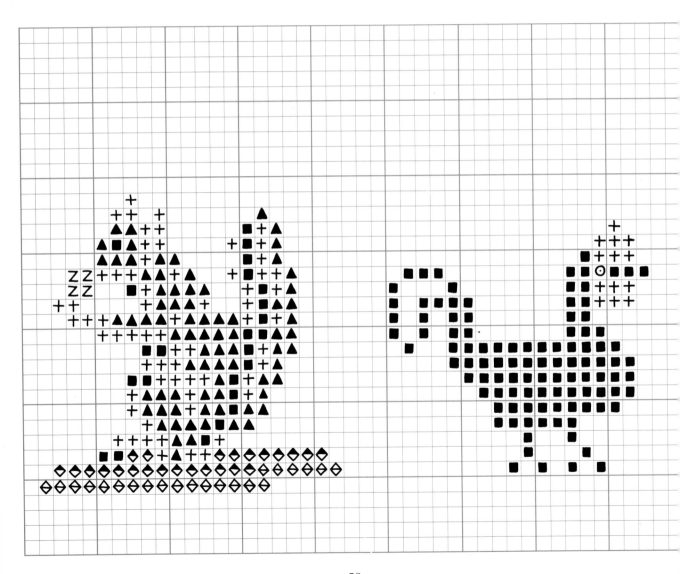

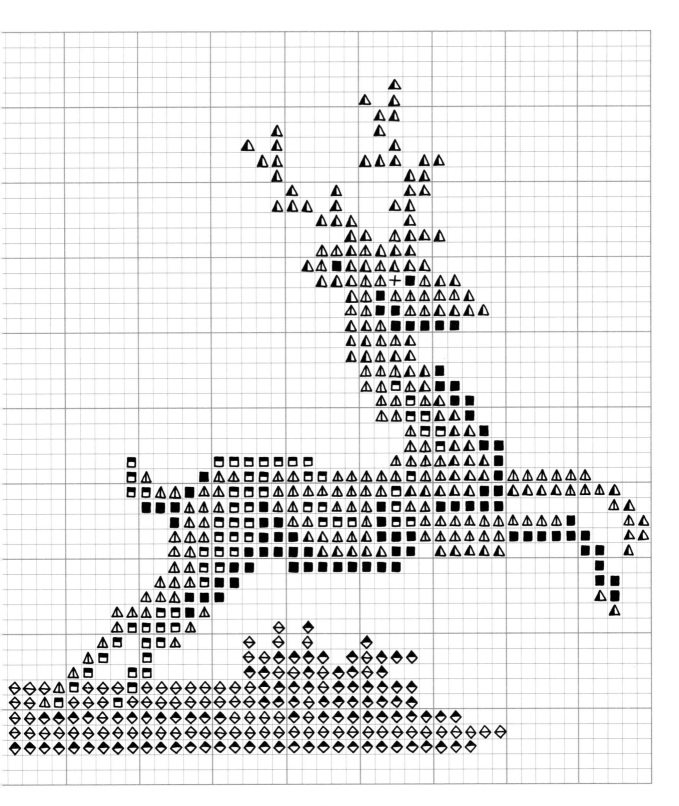

Cat, dogs and hare from 1823
(see cover)

▲ = dark brown (360)   ■ = black (403)

◆ = dark green (246)   ▯ = medium grey (399)

◇ = light green (242)   ▤ = silver grey (397)

+ = red (47)   ▢ = white (402)

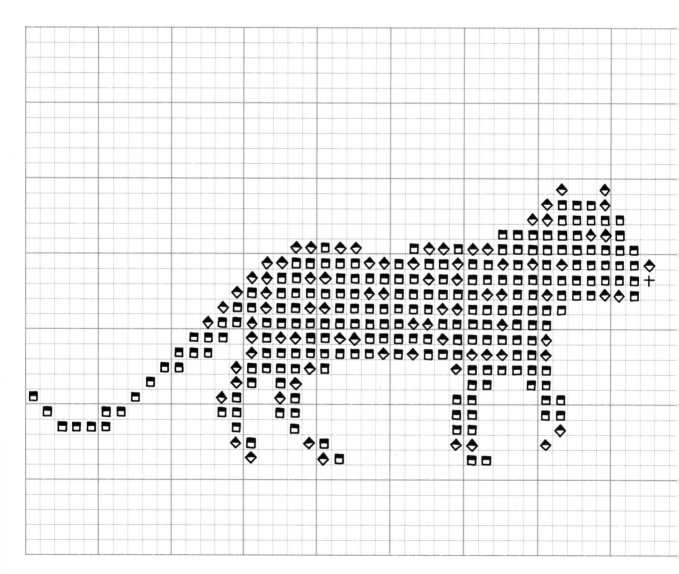

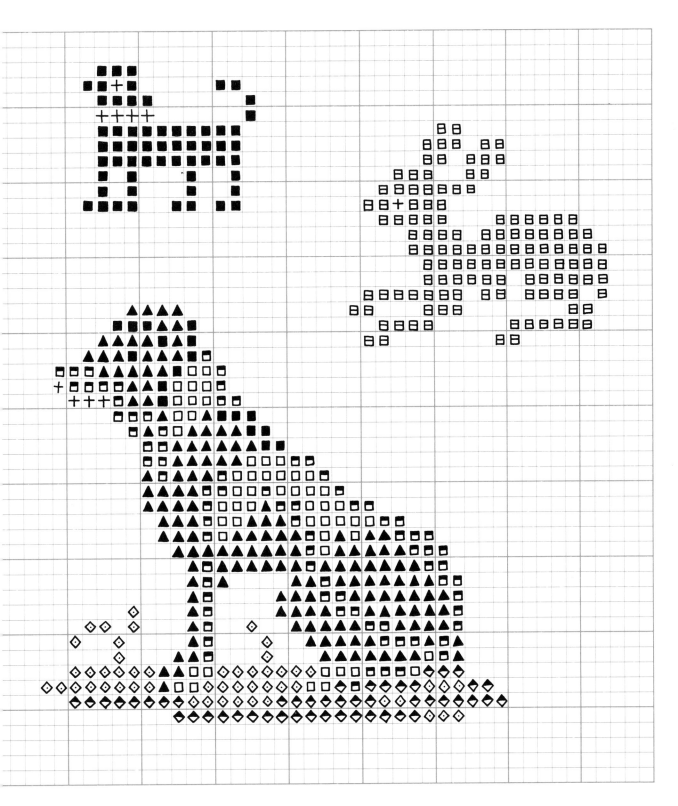

Stork, small
bird and
parrot
motifs from
1823
(see cover)

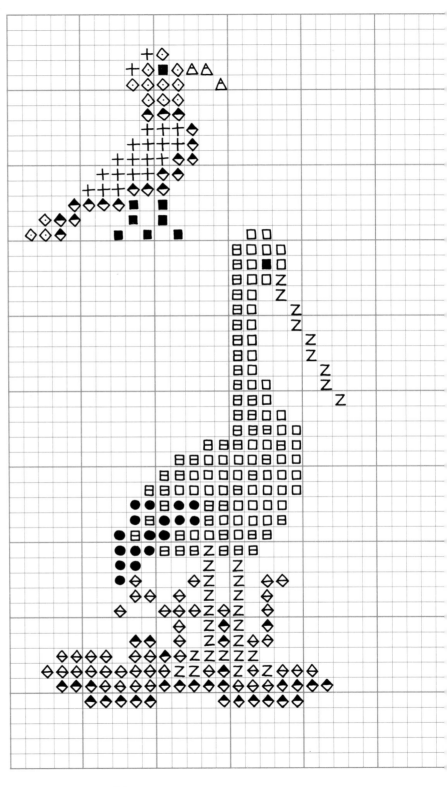

■ = black (403)

▣ = medium grey (399)

目 = silver grey (397)

□ = white (402)

△ = dark yellow (291)

◈ = dark green (246)

◒ = medium green (244)

◇ = light green (242)

◇ = pale green (214)

● = dark blue (135)

+ = red (47)

Z = pink (25)

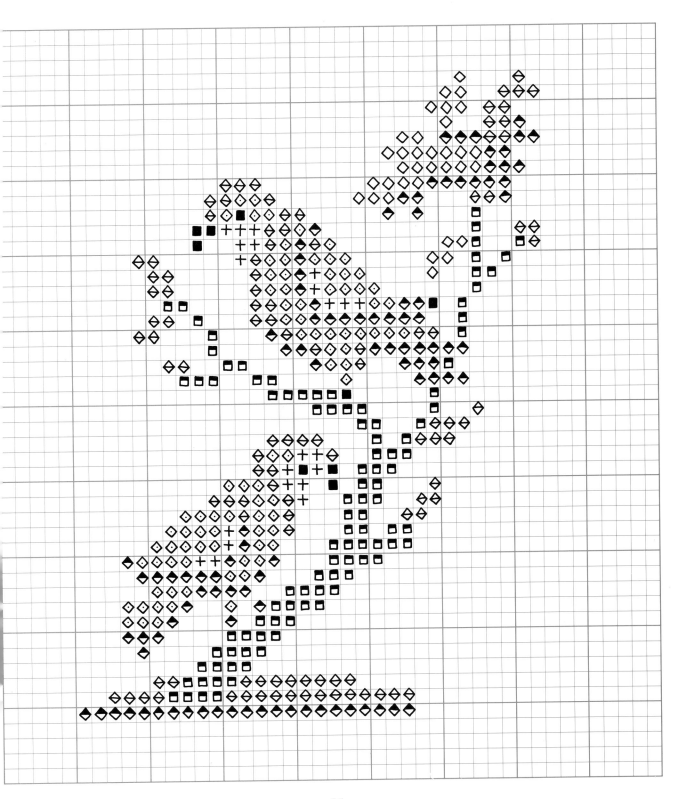

■ = black (403)   △ = yellow (290)

□ = white (402)   ◇ = light green (242)

▲ = medium brown (371)   + = red (47)

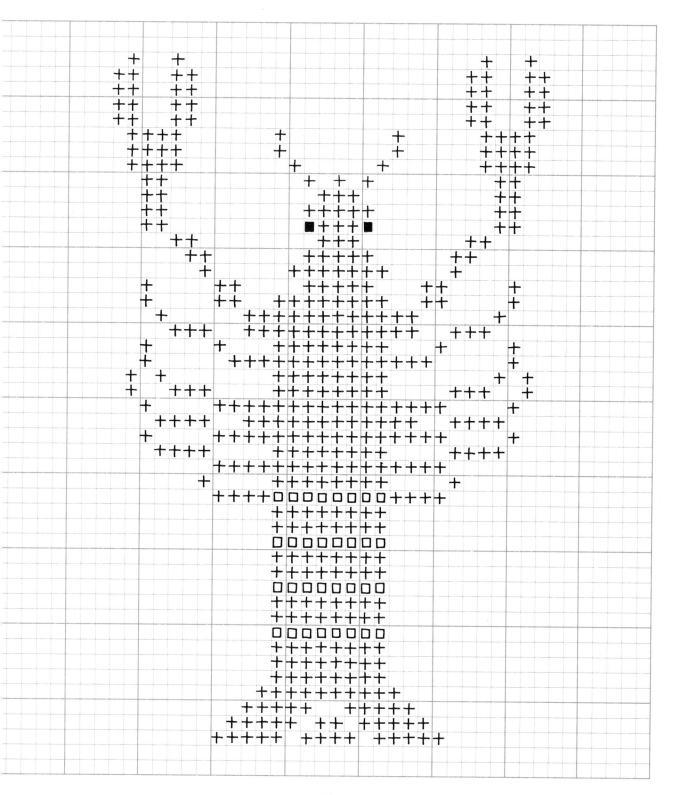

Horn and house from 1823
(see cover)

■ = black (403)
▢ = medium grey (399)
⊡ = light grey (398)
▲ = dark brown (360)
△ = dark yellow (291)
△ = yellow (290)
◆ = dark green (246)
+ = red (47)

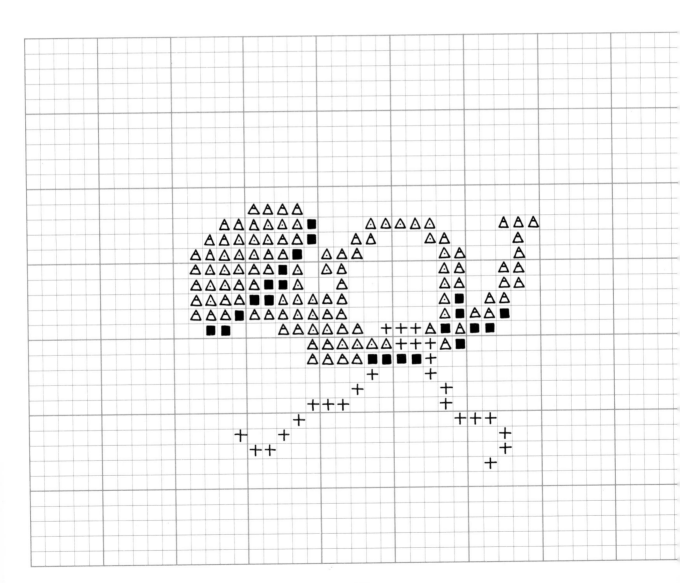

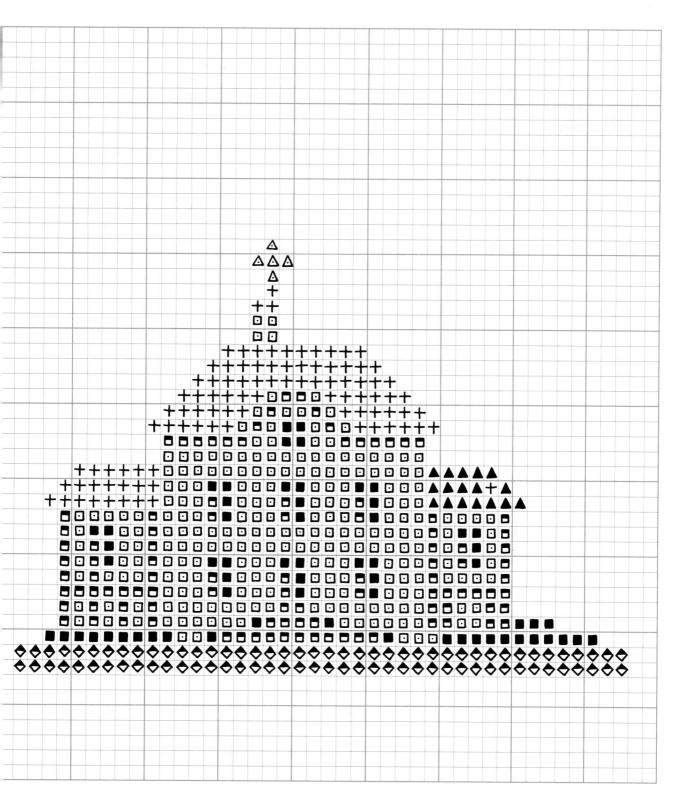

Basket of flowers, flower and wreath of blossoms from 1823

(see cover)

△ = dark yellow (291)	⊙ = light blue (130)
△ = yellow (290)	⊗ = violet (873)
◆ = dark green (246)	+ = red (47)
◈ = medium green (244)	✕ = reddish pink (29)
◇ = light green (242)	Z = pink (25)

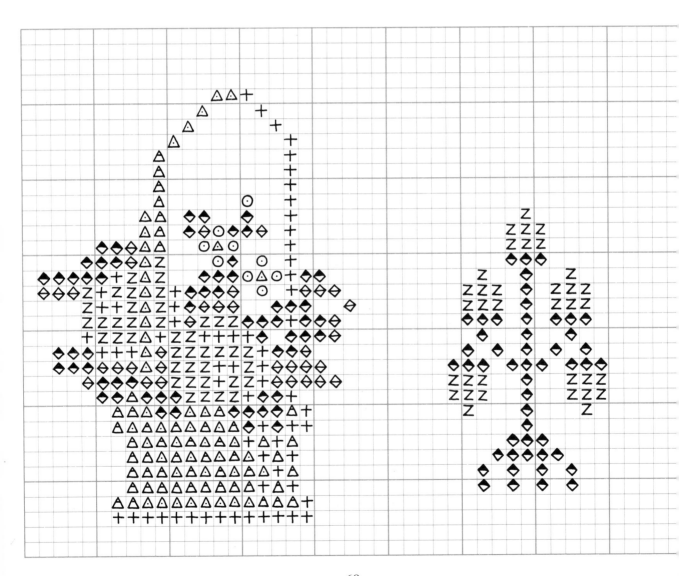

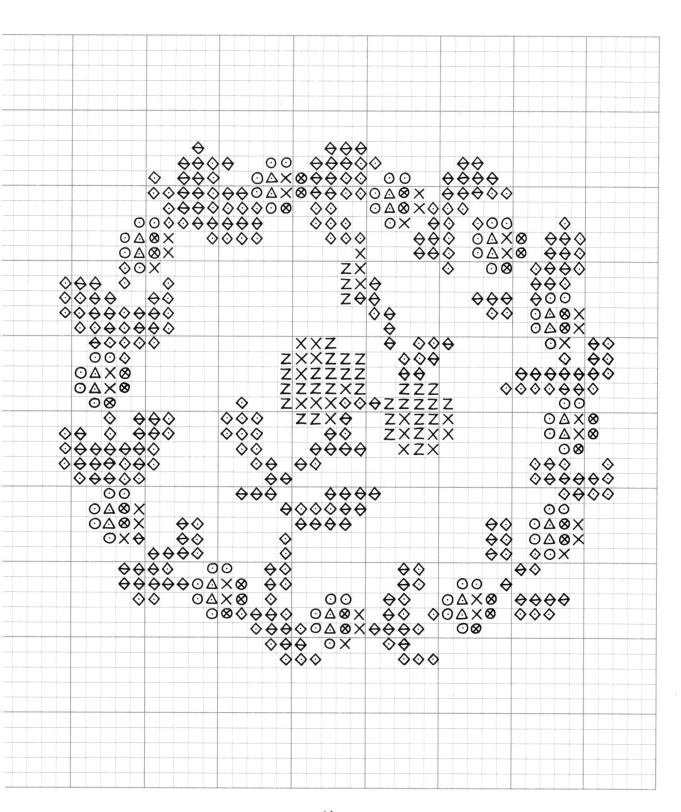

Flower motifs from 1823
(see cover)

Rows of patterns from 1838
(see page 27)

■ = black (403)
△ = medium brown (371)
△ = yellow (290)
◆ = dark green (246)
◈ = medium green (244)
◇ = light green (242)
◇ = pale green (214)

Ⓘ = medium blue (132
⊙ = light blue (130)
○ = pale blue (128)
Z = pink (25)
Y = dusty pink (968)
∧ = pale pink (23)

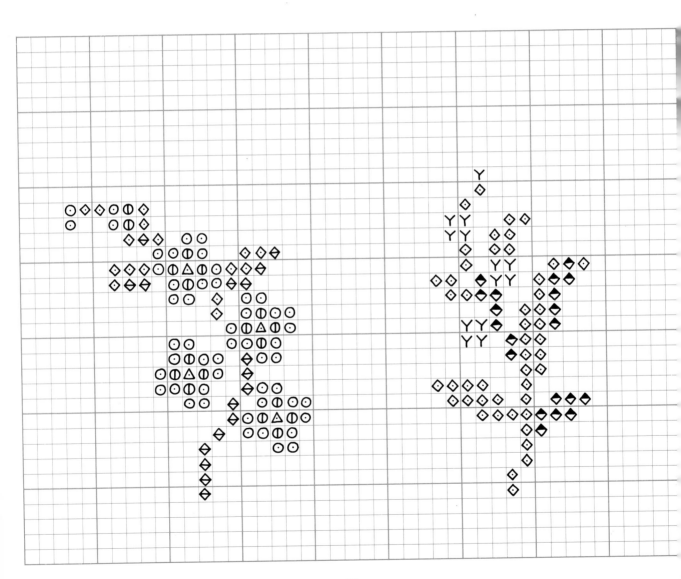

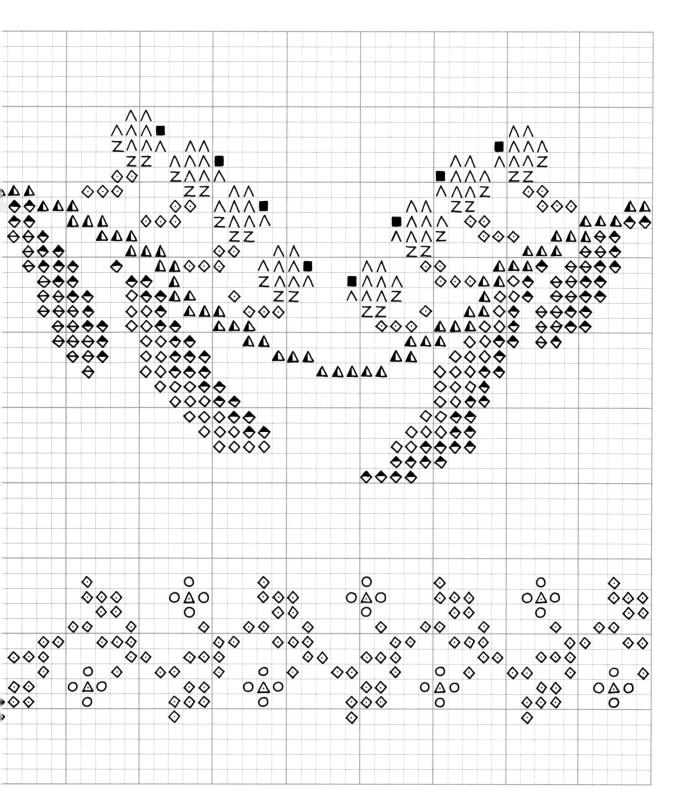

Rose from about 1820
(see page 29)

Anchor and hearts from 1838
(see page 27)

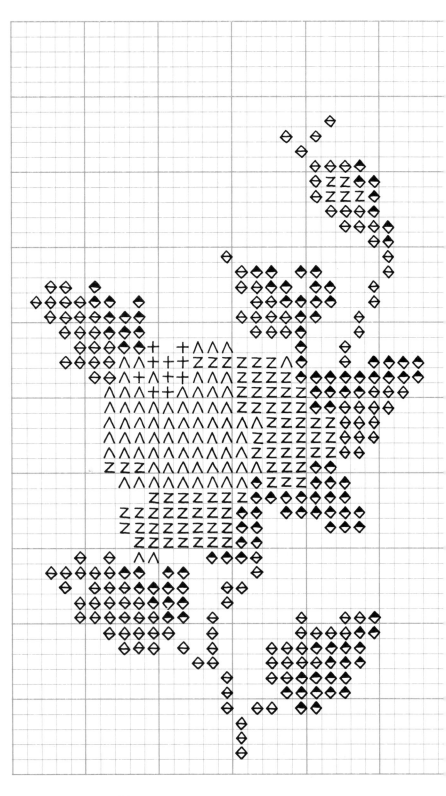

■ = black (403)

▯ = medium grey (399)

⊟ = silver grey (397)

△ = yellow (290)

◆ = dark green (246)

⬥ = medium green (244)

◇ = light green (242)

+ = red (47)

✕ = reddish pink (29)

Z = pink (25)

∧ = pale pink (23)

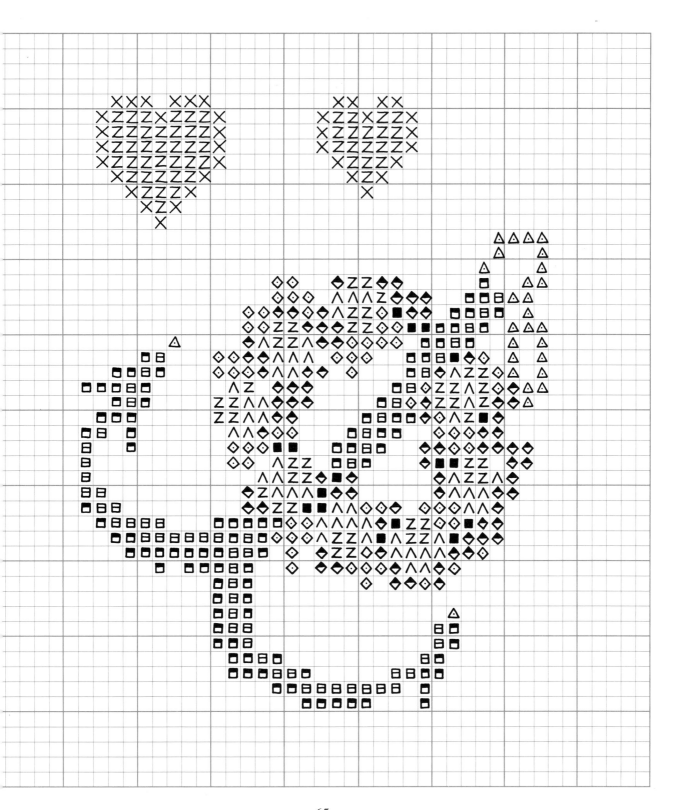

*Row of
patterns from
about 1820*
(see page 29)
*Star from
1838*
(see page 27)

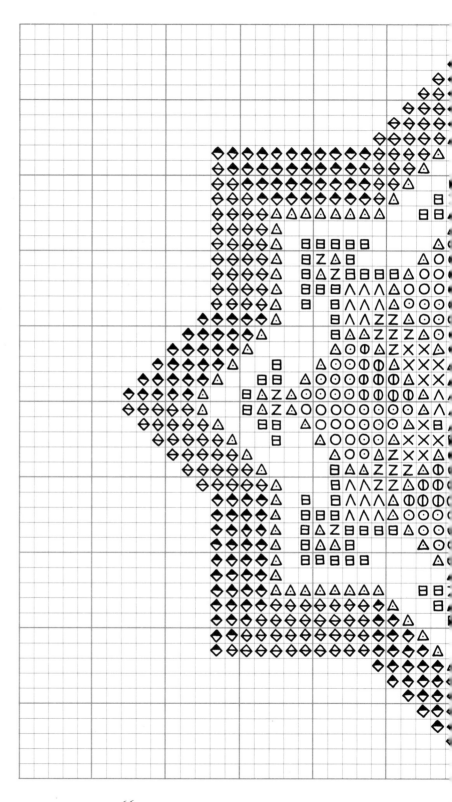

⊟ = silver grey (397)

▲ = dark yellow (291)

△ = yellow (290)

△ = light yellow (288)

◆ = dark green (246)

◈ = medium green (244)

◇ = light green (242)

⏀ = medium blue (132)

☉ = light blue (130)

○ = pale blue (128)

✕ = reddish pink (29)

Z = pink (25)

∧ = pale pink (23)

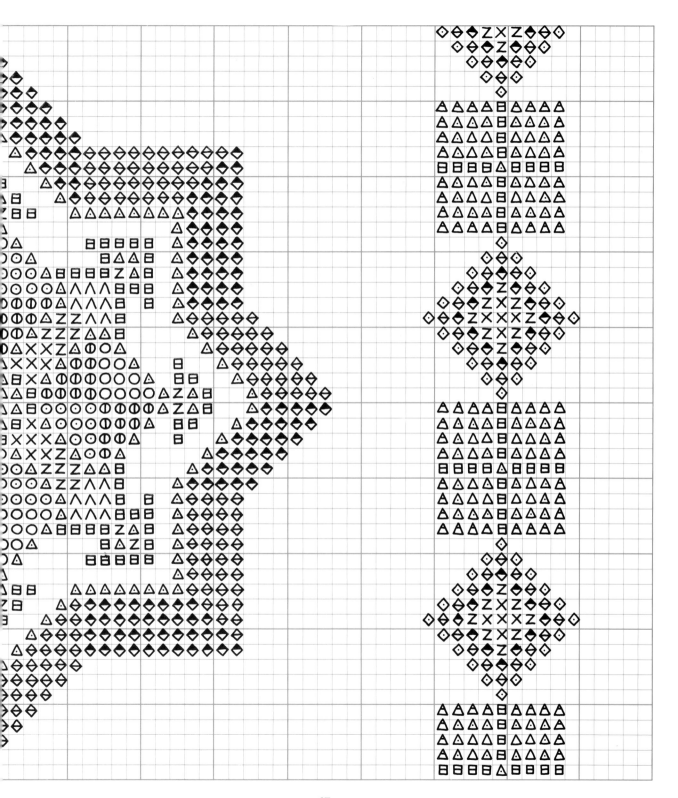

Rows of patterns from 1820–1838
(see pages 27 and 29)

☐ = white (402)   ◐ = medium blue (132)
△ = dark yellow (291)   ☉ = light blue (130)
△ = yellow (290)   + = red (47)
△ = light yellow (288)   X = reddish pink (29)
◆ = dark green (246)   Z = pink (25)
◆ = medium green (244)   ∧ = pale pink (23)
◇ = light green (242)

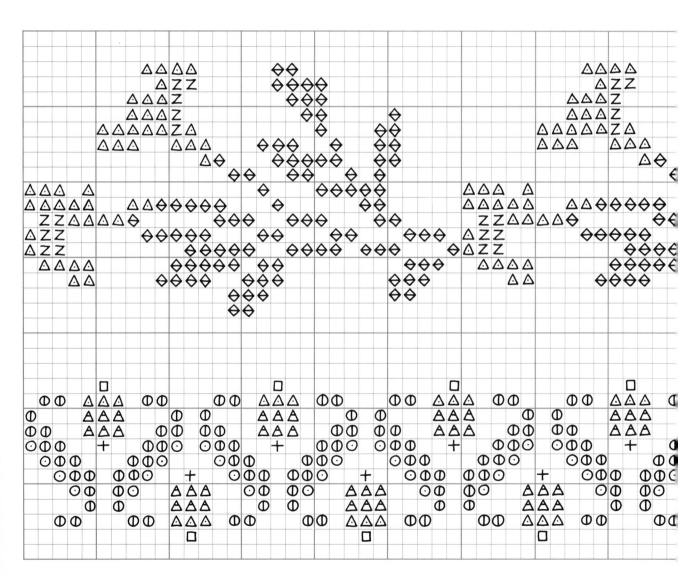

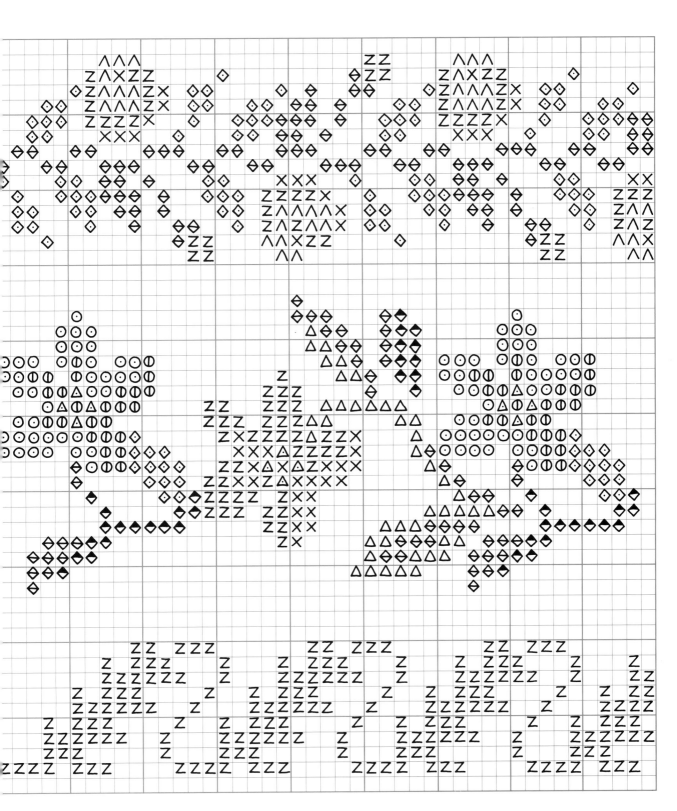

Guitar and rows of patterns from 1842

■ = black (403)	◇ = pale green (214)
⬓ = medium grey (399)	O = pale blue (128)
⊟ = silver grey (397)	⊗ = violet (873)
⧄ = cream (386)	✳ = dark red (20)
⬜ = white (402)	+ = red (47)
△ = yellow (290)	Z = pink (25)
◈ = dark green (246)	Y = dusty pink (968)
◈ = medium green (244)	∧ = pale pink (23)

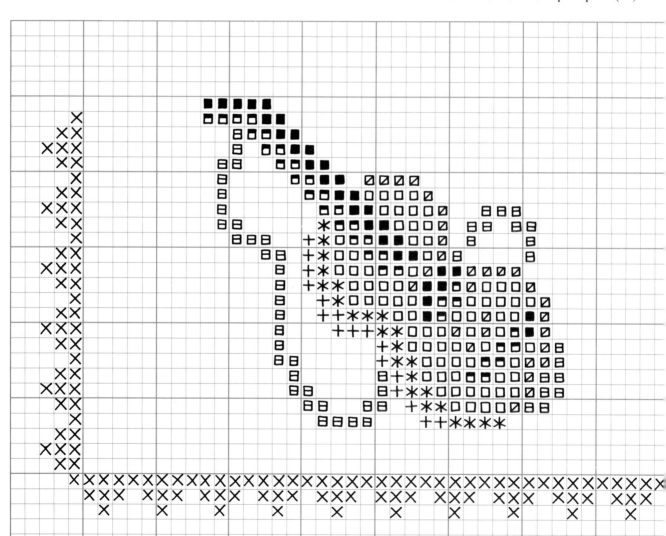

70

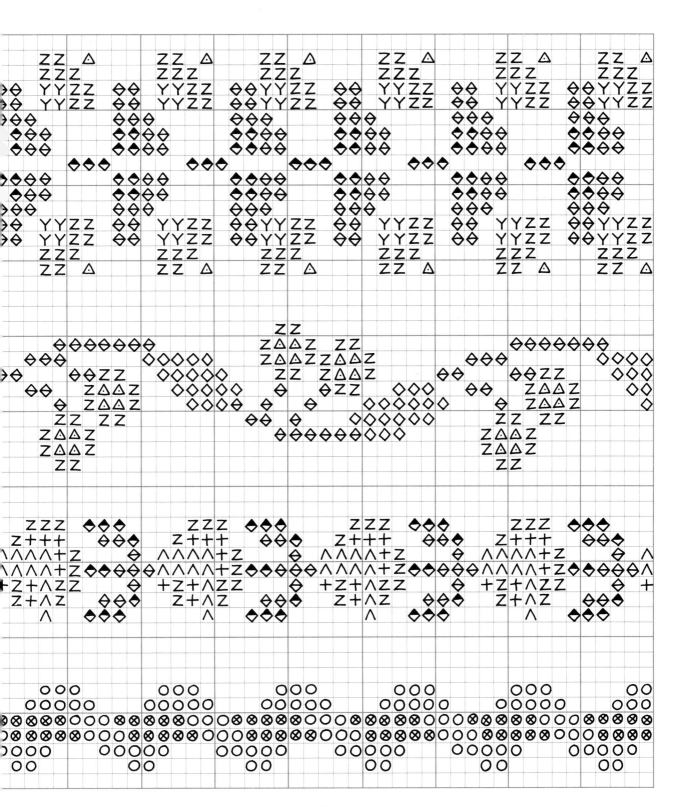

Candle from 1843
Small flowers from 1838
(see page 27)
Coffee pot and coffee grinder
from 1842

■ = black (403)
□ = medium grey (399)
目 = silver grey (397)
▢ = white (402)
▲ = dark brown (360)
◮ = medium brown (371)
⬘ = light brown (369)
◭ = dark yellow (291)
△ = yellow (290)
△ = light yellow (288)

◆ = dark green (246)
⬙ = medium green (244)
◇ = light green (242)
Φ = medium blue (132)
⊙ = light blue (130)
O = pale blue (128)
X = reddish pink (29)
Z = pink (25)
∧ = pale pink (23)

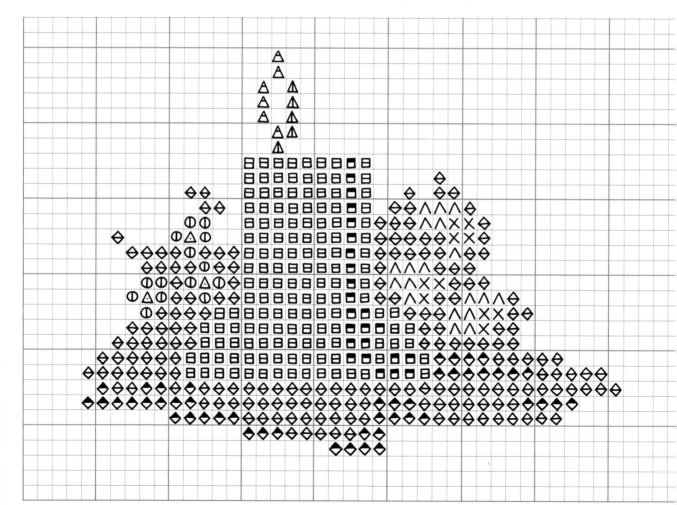

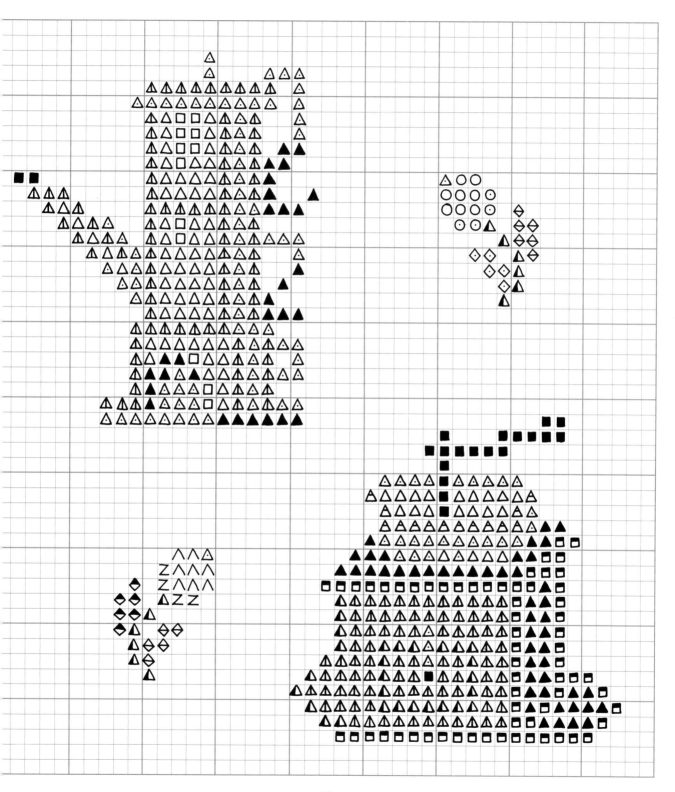

Cornucopia and vase of flowers from 1843
Dove from 1842
Large cornucopia from about 1820
(see page 29)

◨ = dark grey (400)   ◇ = pale green (214)
▣ = medium grey (399)   ⊕ = medium blue (132)
⊟ = silver grey (397)   ⊙ = light blue (130)
□ = white (402)   ⊗ = violet (873)
▲ = medium brown (371)   + = red (47)
◮ = dark yellow (291)   X = reddish pink (29)
△ = yellow (290)   Z = pink (25)
◆ = dark green (246)   Y = dusty pink (968)
⬦ = medium green (244)   Λ = pale pink (23)
◇ = light green (242)

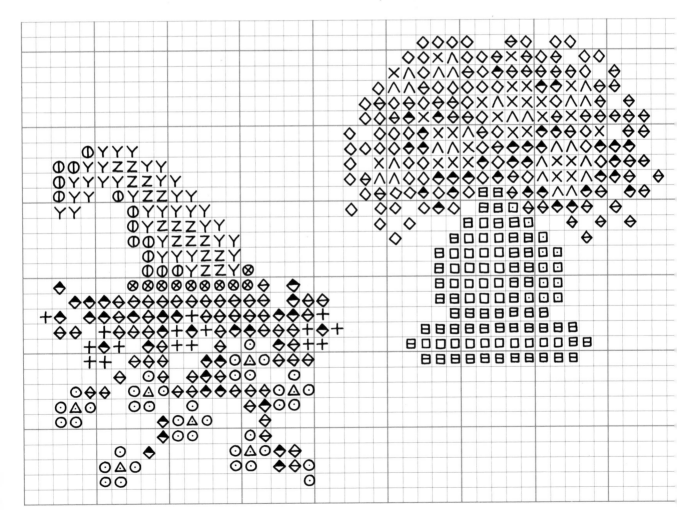

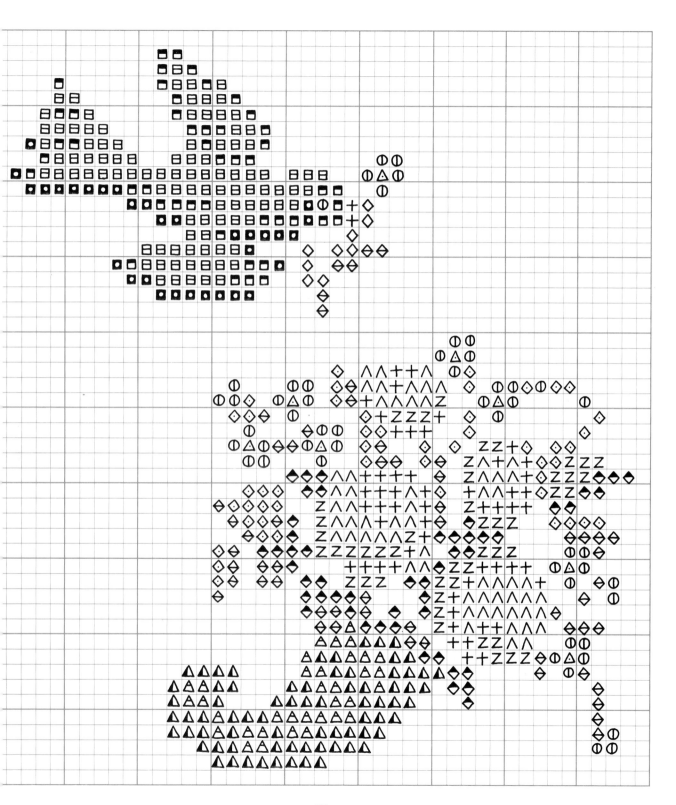

X = colour of your choice

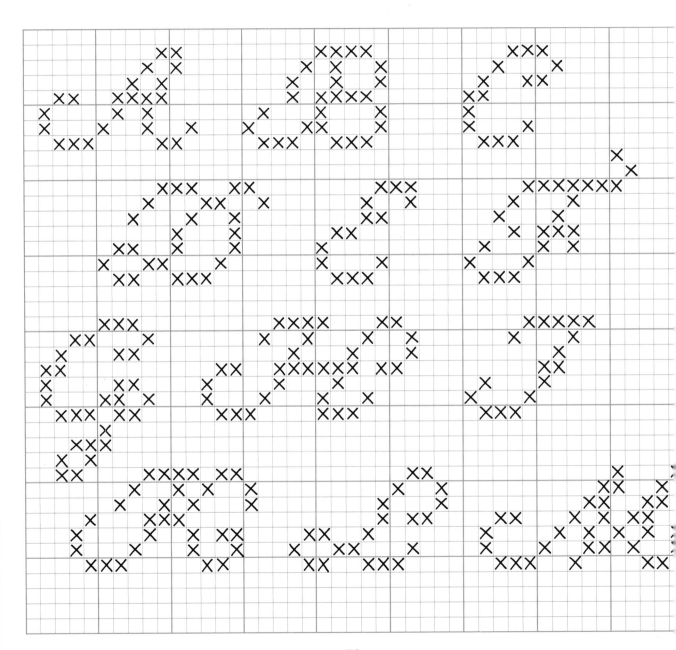

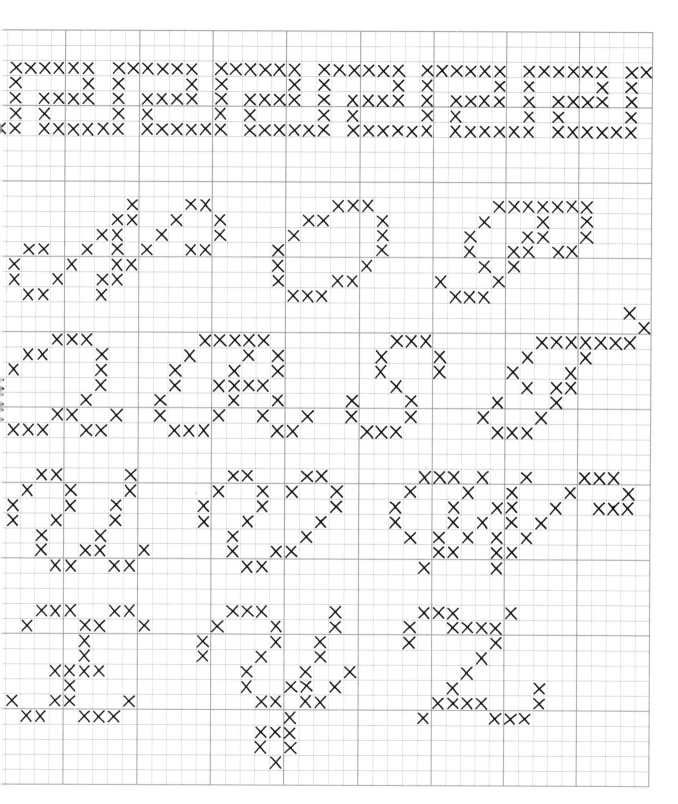

Rows of patterns from 1847
(see page 28)

Friendship motif from 1847
(see page 28)

▢ = dark grey (400)
△ = dark yellow (291)
△ = yellow (290)
◆ = dark green (246)
⬦ = medium green (244)
◇ = pale green (214)
● = dark blue (150)

Φ = medium blue (132)
☉ = light blue (130)
⊗ = violet (873)
+ = red (47)
Z = pink (25)
Y = dusty pink (968)
Λ = pale pink (23)

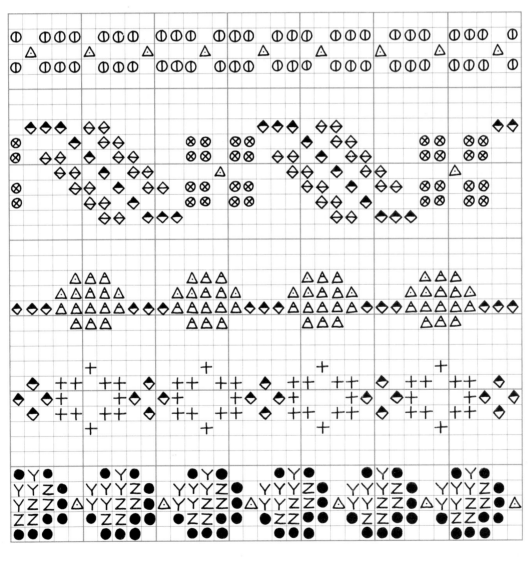

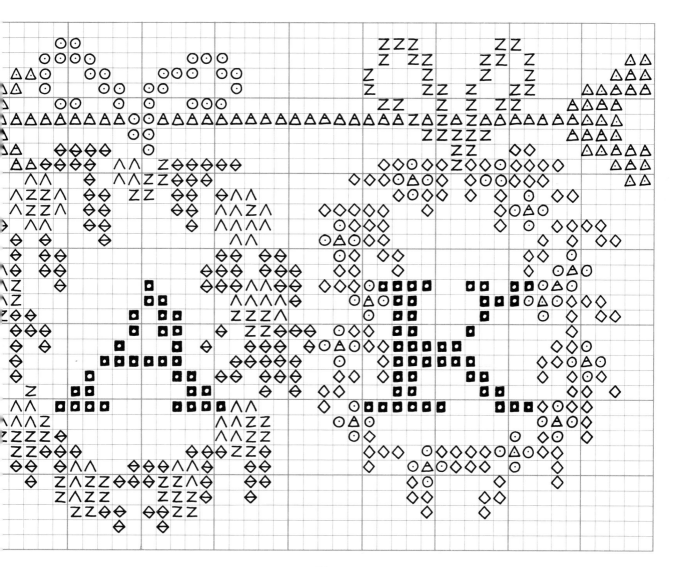

Rows of patterns and fruit bowl from 1847

(see page 28)

△ = dark yellow (291)   O = pale blue (128)

△ = yellow (290)   ⊗ = violet (873)

◈ = dark green (246)   X = reddish pink (29)

◈ = medium green (244)   Z = pink (25)

◇ = light green (242)   ∧ = pale pink (23)

◐ = medium blue (132)

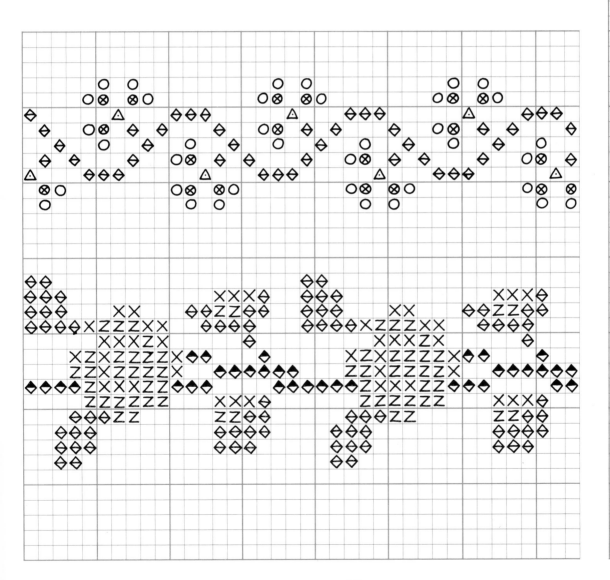

80

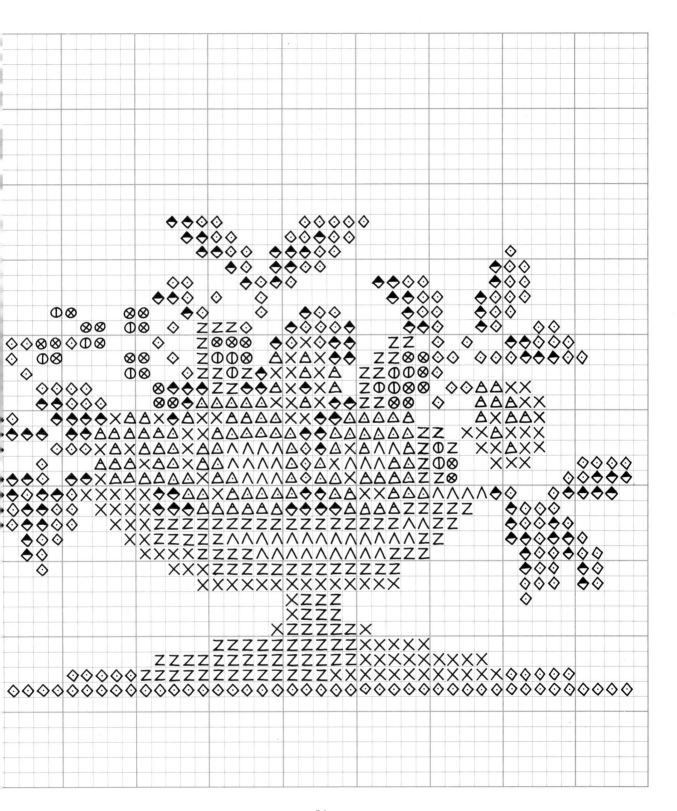

Flowering branch, small flowers and dove with branch from 1847
(see page 28)

■ = black (403)   ◈ = medium green (244)
▣ = medium grey (399)   ◇ = light green (242)
▤ = silver grey (297)   ◇ = pale green (214)
□ = white (402)   ● = dark blue (150)
▲ = dark brown (360)   ◉ = medium blue (132)
△ = medium brown (371)   ⊙ = light blue (130)
△ = dark yellow (291)   ○ = pale blue (128)
△ = yellow (290)   + = red (47)
◆ = dark green (246)

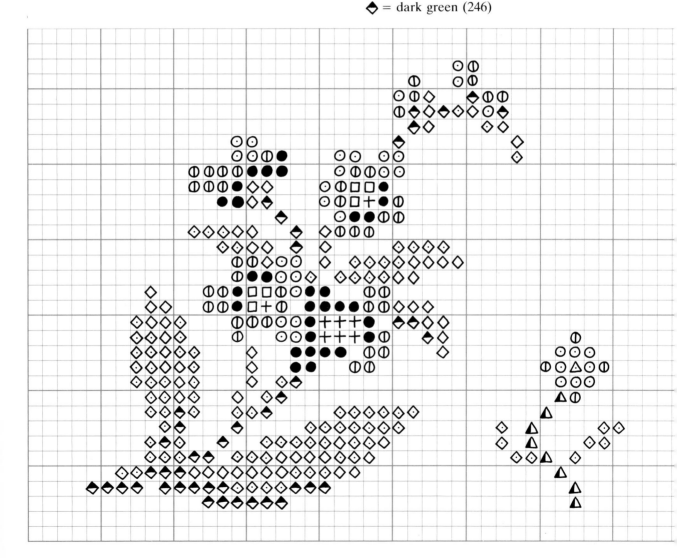

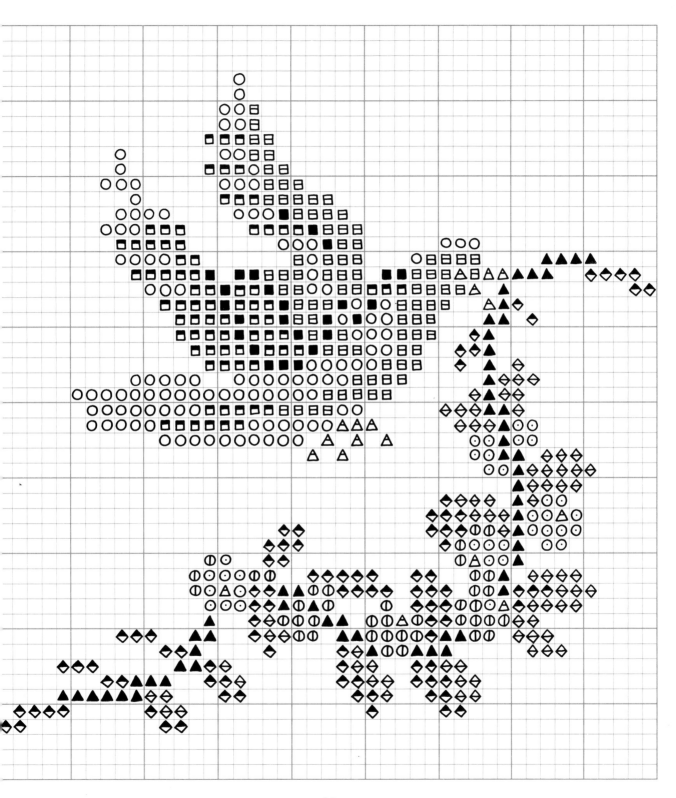

Flower, bird, butterflies and basket of flowers from 1812–1847

(see pages 25, 28 and cover)

■ = black (403) ⊗ = violet (873)
□ = white (402) ✳ = dark red (20)
△ = dark yellow (291) + = red (47)
△ = yellow (290) ✕ = reddish pink (29)
◆ = dark green (246) Z = pink (25)
◇ = medium green (244) Y = dusty pink (968)
◐ = medium blue (132) ∧ = pale pink (23)
⊙ = light blue (130)

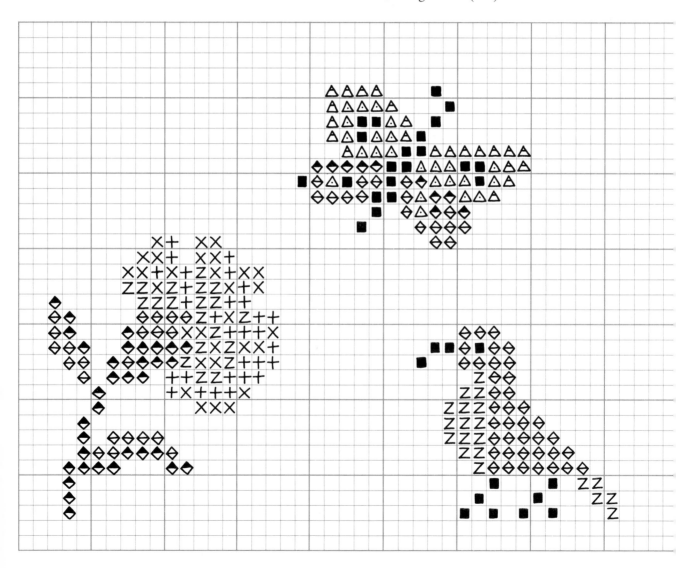

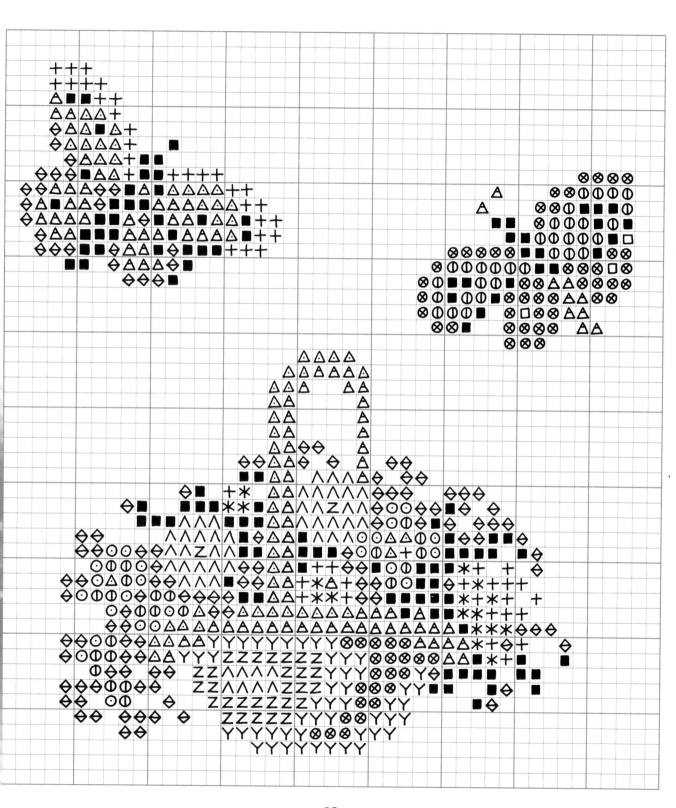

Row of patterns, numerals
and wreath of flowers
from 1847
(see page 28)

△ = dark yellow (291)   ◇ = pale green (214)
△ = yellow (290)   X = reddish pink (29)
◆ = dark green (246)   Z = pink (25)
◇ = light green (242)   ∧ = pale pink (23)

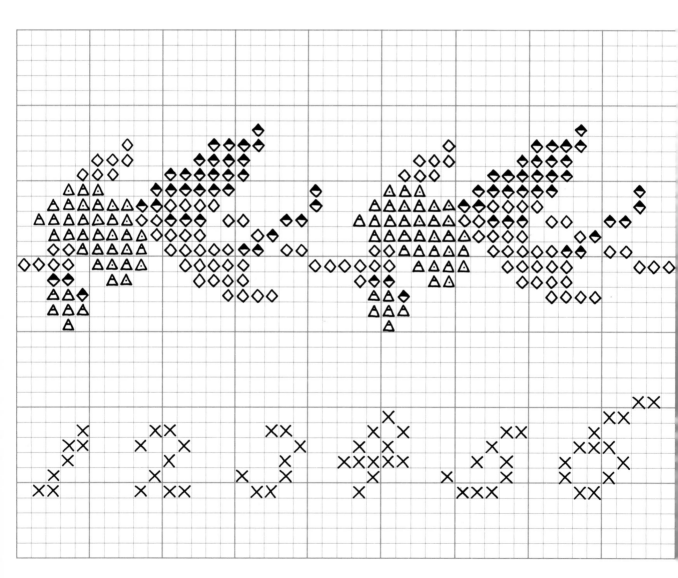

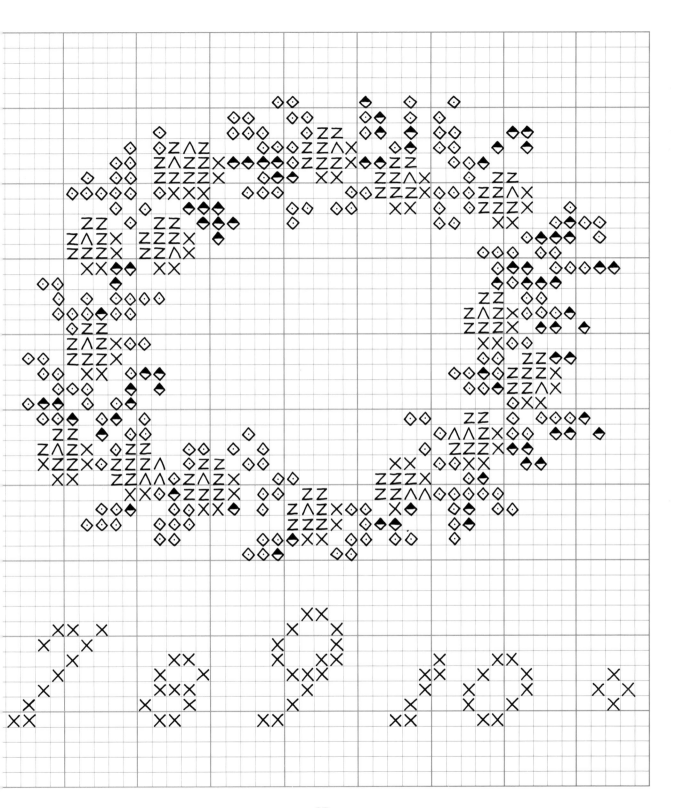

Rows of patterns from 1847
(see page 28)

□ = white (402)　　◆ = dark green (246)
▲ = medium brown (371)　◇ = medium green (244)
△ = yellow (290)　　Z = pink (25)

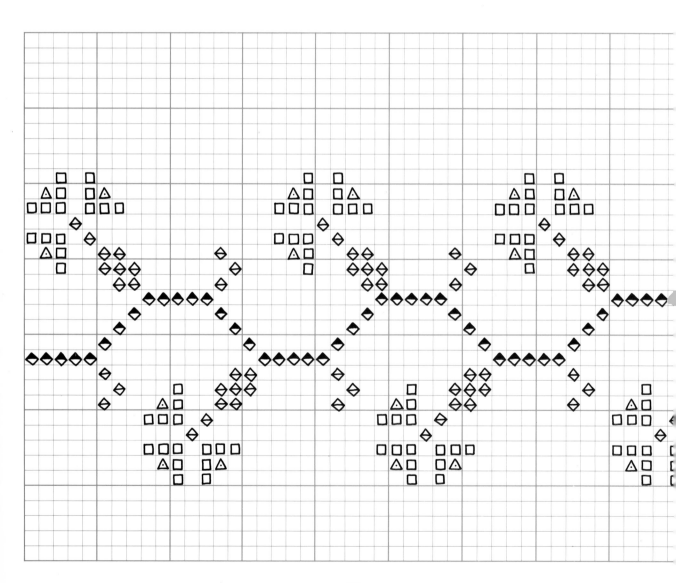

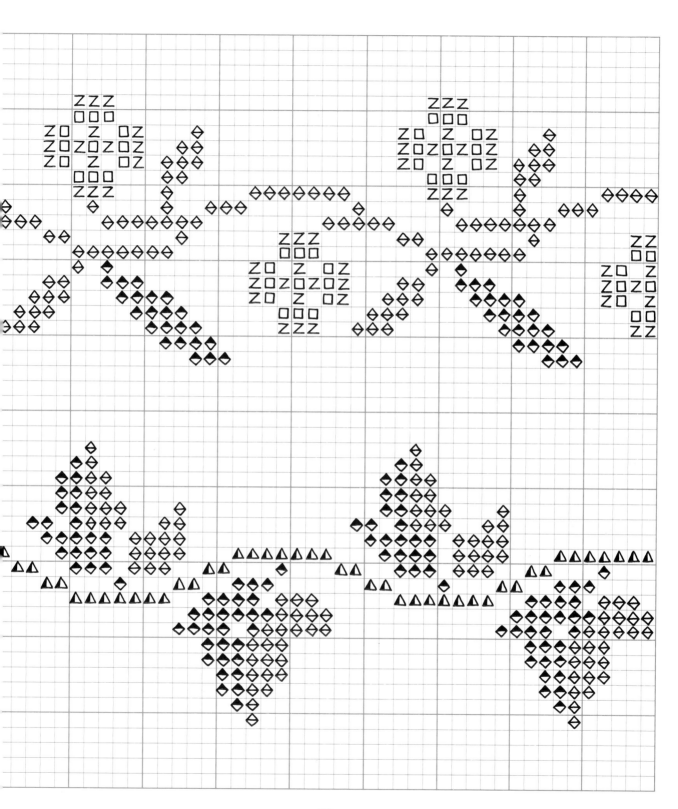

Cornflower and pansy
from 1842
Small tree with birds and
flowering branch from 1812
(see page 25)

■ = black (403)   ◇ = light green (242)

□ = white (402)   ◇ = pale green (214)

▲ = medium brown (371) ● = dark blue (150)

△ = yellow (290)   ◑ = medium blue (132)

◆ = dark green (246)   ○ = pale blue (128)

◈ = medium green (244) ✚ = red (47)

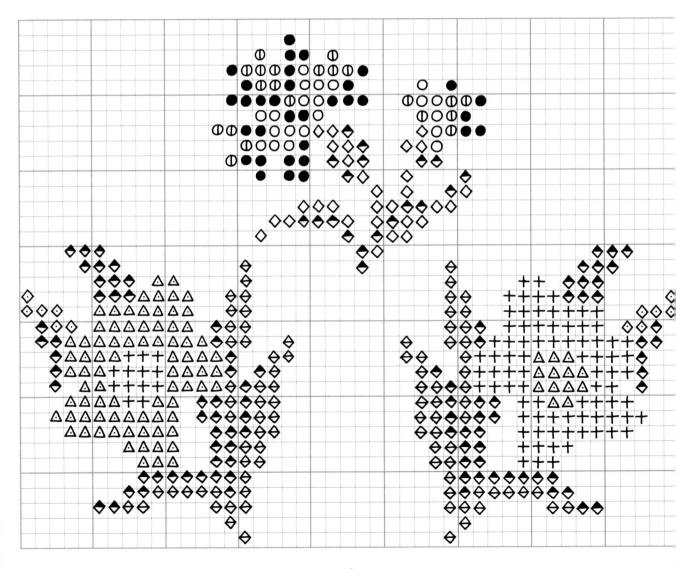

90

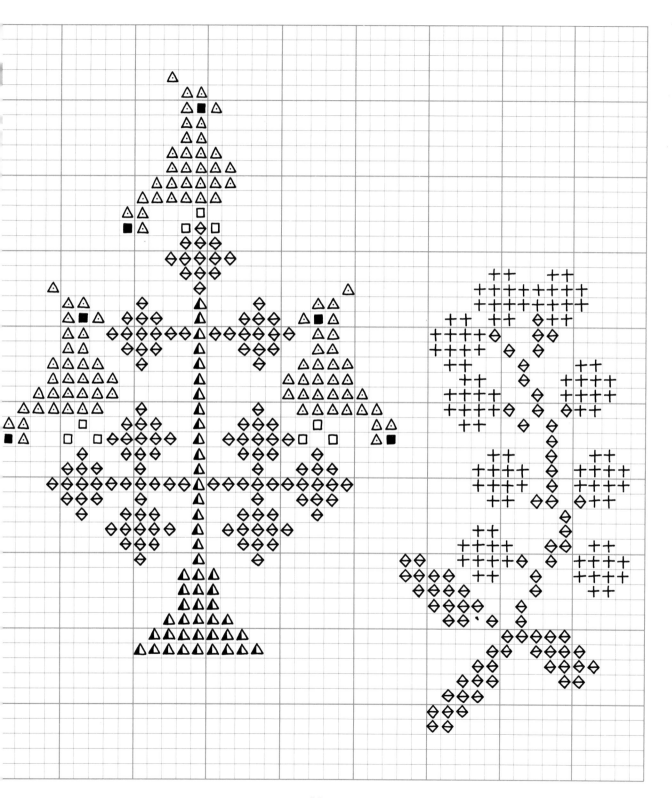

Strawberries and parrot
from 1812
(see page 25)
Puppy

■ = black (403)
▣ = medium grey (399)
□ = white (402)
▲ = dark brown (360)
△ = medium brown (371)
⬭ = light brown (369)

△ = yellow (290)
◆ = dark green (246)
◈ = medium green (244)
Ⓞ = medium blue (132)
+ = red (47)
Z = pink (25)

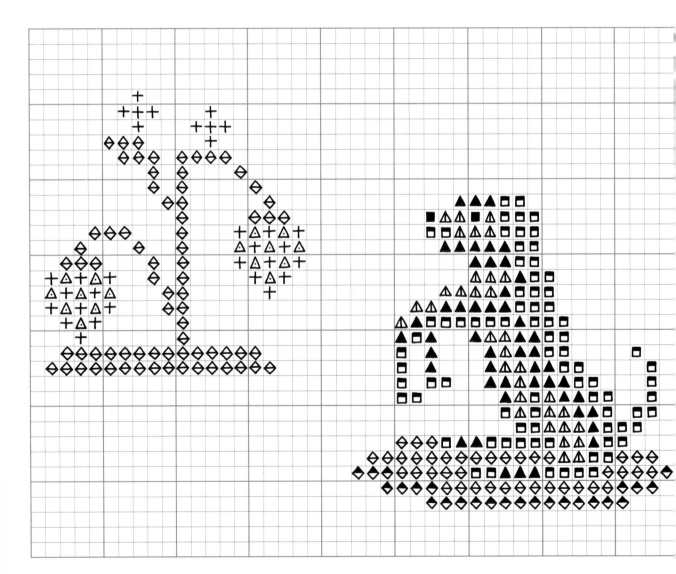

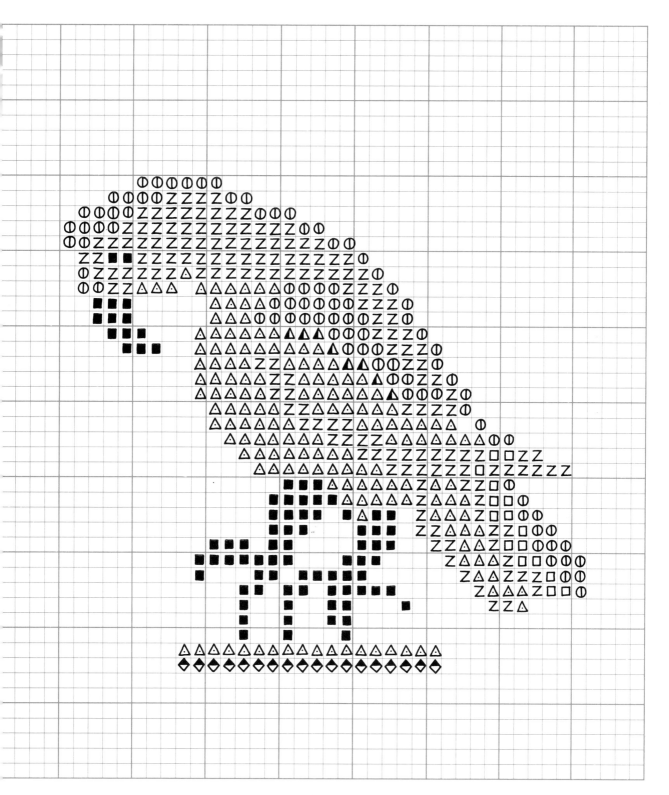

Two rows of patterns and small tree with birds from 1826

■ = black (403)
□ = white (402)
▲ = dark brown (360)
◬ = light brown (369)
△ = yellow (290)
◆ = dark green (246)

◈ = medium green (244)
◇ = light green (242)
⊙ = light blue (130)
+ = red (47)
Z = pink (25)

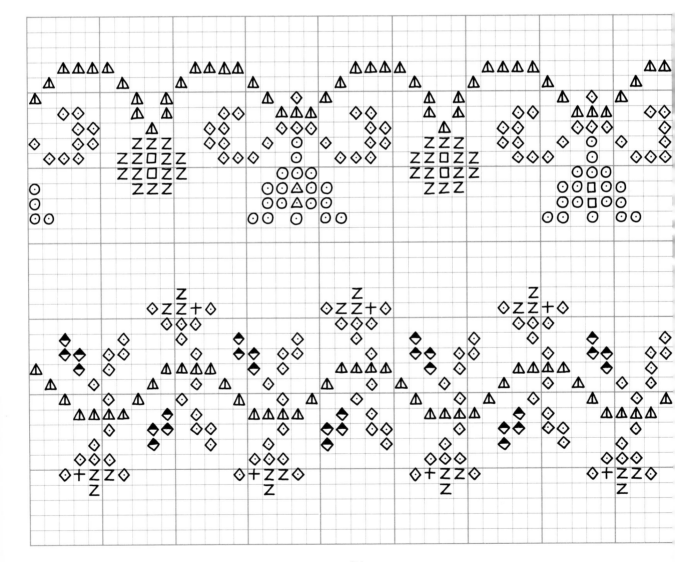

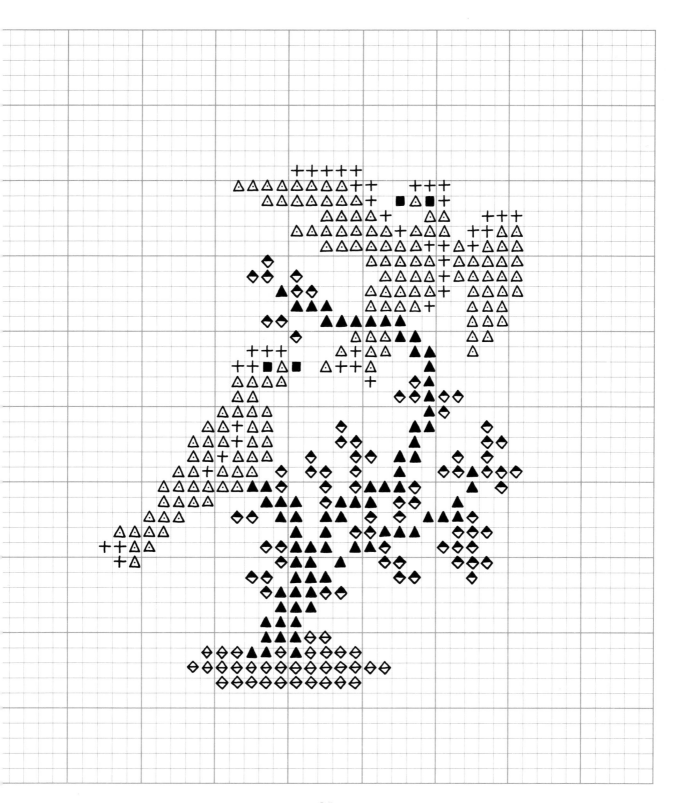

Playing cards from 1838
(see page 27)

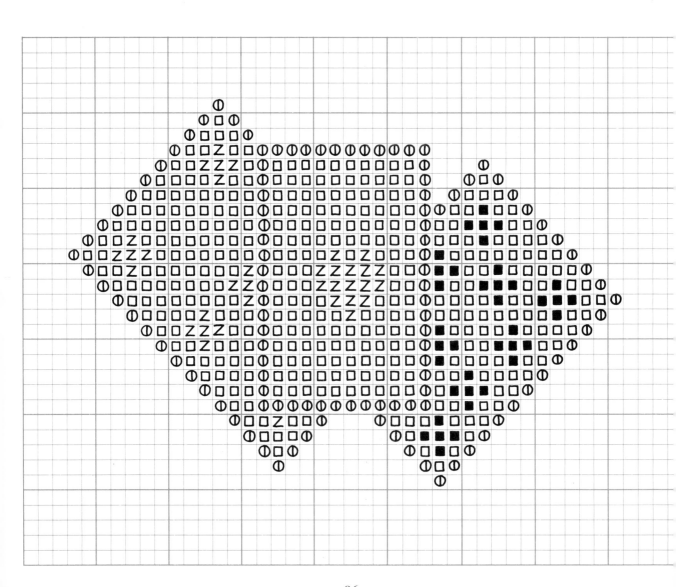